EARLY CHILDHOOD EDUCATION SERIES

Sharon Ryan, Editor

ADVISORY BOARD: Barbara T. Bowman, Harriet K. Cuffaro, Stephanie Feeney, Doris Pronin Fromberg, Celia Genishi, Stacie G. Goffin, Dominic F. Gullo, Alice Sterling Honig, Elizabeth Jones, Gwen Morgan

(continued)

Major Trends and Issues in Early Childhood Education:
Challenges, Controversies, and Insights, 2nd Ed.
  JOAN PACKER ISENBERG & MARY RENCK JALONGO, EDS.

The Power of Projects: Meeting Contemporary
Challenges in Early Childhood Classrooms—
Strategies and Solutions
  JUDY HARRIS HELM & SALLEE BENEKE, EDS.

Bringing Learning to Life: The Reggio Approach to Early
Childhood Education
  LOUISE BOYD CADWELL

The Colors of Learning: Integrating the Visual Arts
into the Early Childhood Curriculum
  ROSEMARY ALTHOUSE, MARGARET H. JOHNSON, &
  SHARON T. MITCHELL

A Matter of Trust: Connecting Teachers and Learners in
the Early Childhood Classroom
  CAROLLEE HOWES & SHARON RITCHIE

Widening the Circle: Including Children with
Disabilities in Preschool Programs
  SAMUEL L. ODOM, ED.

Children with Special Needs: Lessons for Early
Childhood Professionals
  MARJORIE J. KOSTELNIK, ESTHER ETSUKO ONAGA,
  BARBARA ROHDE, & ALICE PHIPPS WHIREN

Developing Constructivist Early Childhood Curriculum:
Practical Principles and Activities
  RHETA DEVRIES, BETTY ZAN, CAROLYN HILDEBRANDT,
  REBECCA EDMIASTON, & CHRISTINA SALES

Outdoor Play: Teaching Strategies with Young Children
  JANE PERRY

Embracing Identities in Early Childhood Education:
Diversity and Possibilities
  SUSAN GRIESHABER & GAILE S. CANNELLA, EDS.

Bambini: The Italian Approach to Infant/Toddler Care
  LELLA GANDINI & CAROLYN POPE EDWARDS, EDS.

Young Investigators: The Project Approach in the
Early Years
  JUDY HARRIS HELM & LILIAN G. KATZ

Serious Players in the Primary Classroom: Empowering
Children Through Active Learning Experiences, 2nd Ed.
  SELMA WASSERMANN

Telling a Different Story: Teaching and Literacy in an
Urban Preschool
  CATHERINE WILSON

Young Children Reinvent Arithmetic: Implications of
Piaget's Theory, 2nd Ed.
  CONSTANCE KAMII

Managing Quality in Young Children's Programs:
The Leader's Role
  MARY L. CULKIN, ED.

The Early Childhood Curriculum, 3rd Ed.
  CAROL SEEFELDT, ED.

Leadership in Early Childhood, 2nd Ed.
  JILLIAN RODD

Inside a Head Start Center
  DEBORAH CEGLOWSKI

Bringing Reggio Emilia Home
  LOUISE BOYD CADWELL

Master Players
  GRETCHEN REYNOLDS & ELIZABETH JONES

Understanding Young Children's Behavior
  JILLIAN RODD

Understanding Quantitative and Qualitative Research in
Early Childhood Education
  WILLIAM L. GOODWIN & LAURA D. GOODWIN

Diversity in the Classroom, 2nd Ed.
  FRANCES E. KENDALL

Developmentally Appropriate Practice in "Real Life"
  CAROL ANNE WIEN

Experimenting with the World
  HARRIET K. CUFFARO

Quality in Family Child Care and Relative Care
  SUSAN KONTOS, CAROLLEE HOWES, MARYBETH SHINN,
  & ELLEN GALINSKY

Using the Supportive Play Model
  MARGARET K. SHERIDAN, GILBERT M. FOLEY,
  & SARA H. RADLINSKI

The Full-Day Kindergarten, 2nd Ed.
  DORIS PRONIN FROMBERG

Assessment Methods for Infants and Toddlers
  DORIS BERGEN

Young Children Continue to Reinvent Arithmetic—3rd
Grade: Implications of Piaget's Theory
  CONSTANCE KAMII WITH SALLY JONES LIVINGSTON

Moral Classrooms, Moral Children
  RHETA DEVRIES & BETTY ZAN

Diversity and Developmentally Appropriate Practices
  BRUCE L. MALLORY & REBECCA S. NEW, EDS.

Changing Teaching, Changing Schools
  FRANCES O'CONNELL RUST

Physical Knowledge in Preschool Education
  CONSTANCE KAMII & RHETA DEVRIES

Ways of Assessing Children and Curriculum
  CELIA GENISHI, ED.

The Play's the Thing
  ELIZABETH JONES & GRETCHEN REYNOLDS

Scenes from Day Care
  ELIZABETH BALLIETT PLATT

Making Friends in School
  PATRICIA G. RAMSEY

The Whole Language Kindergarten
  SHIRLEY RAINES & ROBERT CANADY

Multiple Worlds of Child Writers
  ANNE HAAS DYSON

The Good Preschool Teacher
  WILLIAM AYERS

The Piaget Handbook for Teachers and Parents
  ROSEMARY PETERSON & VICTORIA FELTON-COLLINS

Visions of Childhood
  JOHN CLEVERLEY & D. C. PHILLIPS

Ideas Influencing Early Childhood Education
  EVELYN WEBER

The Joy of Movement in Early Childhood
  SANDRA R. CURTIS

Supporting Boys' Learning

Strategies for Teacher Practice, Pre-K–Grade 3

Barbara Sprung
Merle Froschl
Dr. Nancy Gropper

with

Dr. Noel S. Anderson, Dr. Blythe Hinitz,
Dr. Donna Akilah M. Wright, and Dr. Ahmed Zaman

Teachers College
Columbia University
New York and London

Published by Teachers College Press, 1234 Amsterdam Avenue, New York, NY 10027

Library of Congress Cataloging-in-Publication Data

Sprung, Barbara.
  Supporting boys' learning : strategies for teacher practice, pre-K–grade 3 / Barbara Sprung, Merle Froschl, Nancy Gropper ; with Noel S. Anderson . . . [et al.].
     p. cm.
  Includes bibliographical references and index.
  ISBN 978-0-8077-5104-6 (pbk. : alk. paper) — ISBN 978-0-8077-5105-3 (hardcover : alk. paper) 1. Boys—Education (Elementary) 2. Sex differences in education. 3. Sex differences in education—Social aspects. 4. Language arts. I. Froschl, Merle. II. Gropper, Nancy. III. Title.
  LC1390.S67 2010
  372.18'21--dc22

                                                                                      2010014710

ISBN 978-0-8077-5104-6 (paperback)
ISBN 978-0-8077-5105-3 (hardcover)

Printed on acid-free paper
Manufactured in the United States of America

17   16   15   14   13   12   11   10   8   7   6   5   4   3   2   1

Contents

123/149

Preface

PURPOSE

Supporting Boys' Learning: Strategies for Teacher Practice, Pre-K–Grade 3 is a call to teachers to develop knowledge and strategies to approach teaching boys in ways that build on their strengths, respect their individual development levels, and adhere to principles of child development that place a high priority on positive social-emotional development as a key to school success.

The impetus for this book is the growing body of research that has raised concerns about boys' vulnerability in terms of social-emotional development, referral to special education, and academic success in school, particularly in terms of literacy. Research from the U.S. Department of Education documents that boys score 16 points lower in reading and 24 points lower in writing than girls, and that three-fourths of this gap has opened up by fourth grade.

Since the early 1970s, most work addressing gender equity focused on the well-being of girls. Why did girls in general not seem interested or adept in the areas of science and math? Why did they not exert themselves physically? Why weren't they engaged in sports? It wasn't because girls weren't potentially capable in all those areas. Through socialization practices, teacher and parental expectations, and media messages, girls learned that these areas "were not for them." When researchers, policymakers, teachers, and parents took notice and created strategies, including legislation such as Title IX, it worked. Girls are now taking science and math college-preparatory courses; they have been top Science Competition winners; they tend to be the high school valedictorians; and girls' and women's sports receive worldwide attention.

While all this was happening, it was assumed that boys were doing fine. But, as we now know, that was not the case. The fact is that boys are disengaging from school in alarming numbers, beginning at the earliest levels of education. As we discuss in this textbook, boys are stigmatized with the label "bad boy" that follows them through school; they are being expelled from preschool at rates three times the national K–12 average; and they are shunted off to special education as behavior "problems" unable to be dealt with in the classroom. All the research shows that African American and Latino boys are most at risk. If young boys are "turned off to" or even, shockingly as is the case, "turned out of" education early on, the consequences to them and to society are severe.

The purpose of *Supporting Boys' Learning* is to enable current and future teachers to better understand and meet boys' needs in the classroom. This is not at all to imply that work improving girls' education is done, or that girls' needs should be ignored. Effective gender equity benefits both boys and girls.

A PRACTICAL GUIDE

Supporting Boys' Learning is a practical guide that includes real-life examples from the field, a discussion of the key issues, strategies to improve teaching practices, a reflection on one's practice, and a compilation of key resources. The focus is on the critical developmental early childhood years, by which we mean grades pre-K–3. The material is relevant to female and male teachers alike, though the reality is that only about 4% of early childhood teachers are men.

Supporting Boys' Learning begins with a story for reflection, an anecdote about Jared, a 6-year-old boy in first grade, whose tale raises questions that are at the heart of this textbook.

- What are the consequences for boys of the push-down curriculum, an increasingly academic sit-in-your-seat focused approach to early childhood learning?
- How do a teacher's own gender expectations affect boys' learning?
- How do teachers respond to the energy that boys bring to the classroom?
- What strategies can teachers use to engage boys in active learning?

The book is then divided into seven chapters. Chapter 1, "Critical Issues in the Educational Lives of Boys," presents a comprehensive overview of the growing crisis in boys' education, including a discussion of current research. The following topics are covered: the consequences of viewing boys as "problems" in school; the lack of attention to boys' social-emotional development; the growing literacy gap between boys and girls; the need for boys to engage in active learning through play; and the importance of family and community. Overriding issues that cut across all others are also discussed: the intersection of gender with race, ethnicity, and socioeconomic status; the vast overrepresentation of boys in special education; and the negative effect for boys of the "push-down" curriculum.

Chapters 2–6 delve more deeply into each of the critical issues. The chapters begin with an observation from the field and end with practical strategies and key readings. Questions for further reflection provide a catalyst for promoting understanding of boys' needs.

In Chapter 2, "Boys Are Not the Problem: Reflecting About Boys and Masculinity," there is a discussion of the early roots of sex-role socialization, the effects of the "boy code," and the misuse of the current brain research in terms of gender. Chapter 3, "Social-Emotional Development: A Critical Factor for School Success," looks at the real meaning of "school readiness" and the importance of relational teaching. Chapter 4, "Boys and Literacy: Fostering and Sustaining Literacy Development," discusses how to promote and sustain boys' interest in literacy, how to use observation techniques to uncover students' actual interests, and how to help boys make book selections. Chapter 5, "Active Learning Through Play: Essential Elements for Engaging Boys in Learning," addresses the "crisis" in early childhood education and urges a return to the basics of a play-centered curriculum. Chapter 6, "School, Family, and Community Partnerships: Key to Boys' Success in School," discusses the need for positive school/family connections, for viewing parents and other family members as assets, for cultural/lingual respect, and for community support.

Chapter 7, "Observing and Recording Children's Behavior," provides a description of three different methods that can help reveal the role of gender in young children's interactions with adults and other children in classroom settings. These methods—running records, sociograms, and checklists—help teachers explore and reflect on the role that stereotypes, as well as their own expectations about gender, affect young boys' behavior, choice of activities, and interactions with peers.

Various resources are included in the Appendixes: selected reference books on children's literature, quality books geared to boys' interests, and books that can create opportunities to engage boys in discussions about their emotions. A bibliography, referencing the current research and literature used in the development of *Supporting Boys' Learning* also is included, as well as an index.

And, finally, "sidebars " appear throughout the book, in the form of text boxes. In Chapter 1 they highlight research findings; in other chapters they are anecdotes that illustrate typical issues that boys face in school.

LOOKING TO THE FUTURE

Starting in early childhood, and extending through the school experience, broadly shared stereotypes about masculinity impede boys' development in many areas. We believe that if teachers focus on boys' needs and if classroom practice intentionally counters prevalent stereotypes about boys, this will, ultimately, foster a more successful school experience for boys and girls alike. *Supporting Boys' Learning* has been written with this objective in mind.

Acknowledgments

Supporting Boys' Learning grows out of The Raising and Educating Healthy Boys Project, which began in 2000 and is an initiative of the Educational Equity Center at AED. As with all projects, this one would not have been possible without the support of visionary funders who, in this case, recognized the importance of addressing the critical issue of boys' development beginning in early childhood. For this foresight, we are grateful to Luba Lynch, executive director of the A. L. Mailman Family Foundation, and Susan Wefald, director of institutional planning at the Ms. Foundation for Women. We also wish to thank Deborah B. Breznay, executive director, and Henry L. Berman, president of the Edith Glick Shoolman Children's Foundation for their support of our work.

The Project also is indebted to Craig Flood who, as a father and equity professional, has been concerned with the negative effect of gender socialization on young boys since the 1980s. His early work on the issue helped to inspire and launch the Project.

As a first step, the Project conducted a series of focus groups with pre-K–3 teachers and parents in both urban and suburban settings to learn how boys are perceived and to explore strategies for change. The focus groups were conducted in English and in Spanish, when needed. We would like to thank all the teachers and parents who participated for generously and honestly sharing their ideas. They made it clear that, although they were well aware that boys are not faring well in school, strategies for change were scattered at best.

In 2004, the Project held an invitational meeting that brought together a national group of researchers and educators to address the situation of boys' development and school performance. We acknowledge their broad range of expertise, which continues to inform our work and helped to frame the issues in *Supporting Boys' Learning*. They include: Jane Andrias, educational consultant; Denise Glyn Borders, senior vice president and group director, AED; Judy Chu, research scientist and lecturer, Stanford

University; Linda Colón, program manager, Educational Equity Center at AED; Barbara D. Finberg (now deceased), vice president, MEM Associates; Walter S. Gilliam, assistant professor of Child Psychiatry and Psychology, Yale University Study Center; Nancy Nevarez, program officer, AED; Michelle Porche, research scientist, Wellesley Centers for Women; Oralia Puente, senior associate, MSI—Management Systems, Inc.; Miriam Raider-Roth, assistant professor, University at Albany, SUNY; and Susan Shaffer, deputy director and director of Gender Equity Programs, Mid-Atlantic Equity Center.

As a result of the meeting, *Raising and Educating Healthy Boys: A Report on the Crisis in Boys' Education* was issued. It reflected the consensus that there is, indeed, a growing crisis in boys' education, and that early childhood, a high-risk time for boys, is an opportune time to intervene. It was agreed that this issue needed to be addressed on many fronts; an important one being teacher education and training. Once again, we are grateful to Luba Lynch of the A. L. Mailman Family Foundation, who supported the next phase of the Project, entitled "Addressing the Growing Crisis in Boys' Education Through Early Childhood Pre-service Teacher Education," which became known as the Teacher Education Working Group.

The Working Group represented a broad range of teacher education institutions. We are indebted to the hard work, insight, experience, passion, and commitment of this group of educators. They include Dr. Noel S. Anderson, associate professor, Department of Political Science and (with permission) School of Education, Brooklyn College; Dr. Blythe Hinitz, professor, Department of Elementary and Early Childhood Education, College of New Jersey; Dr. Donna Akilah M. Wright, professor, Department of Education, Medgar Evers College, City University of New York; and Dr. Ahmed Zaman, associate professor, early childhood education, Borough of Manhattan Community College, City University of New York.

The Working Group met from 2006 to 2008. During this time, the group developed teacher education "modules," which they piloted and field tested with their own students. These modules, along with the classroom experiences of the members of the group, served as the conceptual underpinnings for the material in *Supporting Boys' Learning*.

We also want to thank Linda Colón, program manager of the Educational Equity Center at AED, who was a valuable participant in the group discussions and who set up a Web site that facilitated group communications and provided resources that informed the work.

We would like to thank the undergraduate students at the College of New Jersey for sharing their research on the crisis in boys' education. We are also indebted to Dick Feldman, Judy Leipzig, Sal Vascellaro, and Karen Weiss, colleagues from Bank Street College, for their insights about the centrality of children's literature in the development of literacy. In addition, we want to thank Bank Street students whose efforts in learning to observe and record were the basis for many of the anecdotes included here. We also acknowledge Amy Weng of the Educational Equity Center at AED for her invaluable help in formatting the manuscript.

Finally, we want to thank Marie Ellen Larcada, our editor at Teachers College Press. Her support, enthusiasm, and skillful editing brought our vision to reality.

A Story for Reflection

Jared is a 6-year-old boy who has just begun first grade. He lives alone with his mother and has regular contact with his father, who lives nearby. His mother works, but the family is eligible for the free/reduced-cost lunch provided by the school. The following is a typical daily schedule for the class:

8:30–9:15	Morning meeting
9:15–10:00	Writer's workshop
10:00–10:45	Reader's workshop
10:45–11:30	Art, music, or dance on M,W,F; small-group work on math and reading on T, Th
11:30–12:15	Lunch/recess
12:15–1:00	Read-aloud or literacy mini-lessons
1:00–1:45	Math
1:45–2:15	Social studies
2:15–3:00	Work time on M, F; gym on W; math, social studies on T, Th

Thus, the major portion of the day is devoted to teacher-directed academic activities. Some are conducted as whole-group mini-lessons. In others, students work either in small groups, pairs, or individually. Opportunities to engage in large-motor physical activities only occur on the days that there is dance or music and on those days when the children get to go outside for recess. Opportunities to engage in self-initiated, open–ended activities using materials such as blocks and manipulatives are offered only twice a week for 45 minutes during the work times at the end of the day.

Jared has been observed to be most active and involved during gym, work time, and art. During academic activities, he often seems distracted and unfocused, and has been observed to fall asleep during teacher-directed mini-lessons.

The following observation occurred during a literacy mini-lesson on topic sentences that began immediately after the children returned from lunch. Because it was raining that day, there was no outdoor recess and the children went to the auditorium after lunch and watched a cartoon.

Jared is sitting cross-legged on the floor in his assigned place in the meeting area directly in front of the teacher. He slumps his body forward and leans against the teacher's chair as she starts to speak. He then turns sideways away from the teacher and leans his upper body forward, resting on his elbows, which are now on the floor. His legs remain crossed, as expected during meeting time, forcing his body to be twisted awkwardly at the waist. His eyes are open, but it looks like he is about to fall asleep.

The teacher notices how he is sitting and stops the lesson. She looks down at him sternly and says, "Oh, dear! Jared, you need to open your ears. You are *not* going to take a nap in my classroom."

The room is silent and Jared does not look up at the teacher. He slowly raises the top part of his body and sits up so that his body is now turned toward the teacher, although his eyes are still on the carpet. His shoulders are slumped.

The teacher resumes the mini-lesson, which continues for about 2 minutes. She then tells the class to return to their seats. All of the students get up, except for Jared. The teacher says, "Jared, did you hear what I just said? Are you listening?" He does not respond. "I didn't hear an answer, Jared." He continues to stare at the carpet and still does not respond. The teacher stares at him and then sighs deeply. She then tells him to get up and step outside the classroom with her. He stands up slowly, continuing to look down. He walks toward the door of the classroom and the teacher follows.

CHAPTER 1

Critical Issues in the Educational Lives of Boys

I'm thinking of one child in particular who was really an intelligent, sweet, good natured child, but in kindergarten somehow was labeled as a bad kid and sat at a separate table (not at group tables with other children). And I could see the self-fulfilling prophecy happening. He was being told he was a bad child, so he started to act that way. (Barbarin & Crawford, 2006, p. 81)

An elementary school teacher once expressed her worst nightmare as "a class of all boys." Clearly, this person brought attitudes and expectations into her classroom that defined boys as troublesome and difficult to teach. How and where did she form her ideas? Did they start way back with the silly rhyme, "What are little boys made of? Snips and snails and puppy dog tails?" Did they come from experience in her classroom? Was she unable to "control" the boys in her class? Was she frightened by this lack of control? Did she view the energy that boys typically brought with them to school as a deterrent to learning?

BOYS ARE NOT THE PROBLEM

Research shows that, all too often, boys are viewed as "problems" in school, and that this perception begins with teachers at the preschool level. The startling findings from a national study showed that pre-kindergarten students are expelled from school at a rate more than three times more often than K–12 students; that boys are five times more likely to be expelled than girls; and that African American boys are most at-risk for expulsion (Gilliam, 2005). African American boys also are stigmatized by teachers beginning in pre-K, and that label often is passed along from teacher to teacher throughout the child's schooling. The label as a "bad

3

Expulsions from preschool occur three times more often than the national K–12 expulsion rate, and boys are five times as likely to be expelled as girls. African American boys are three times more likely to be expelled than white children (Gilliam, 2005).

boy" or "troublemaker" leads to isolation, exclusion from classroom activities, and, most disturbingly, is picked up by the other children and perceived as truth (Barbarin & Crawford, 2006).

Active boys are not finding encouragement in the early childhood and elementary school classroom. Although the energy that boys bring to a classroom should be viewed as an asset, young boys' physical response styles and kinetic learning behaviors are often seen as deficits (Gartrell, 2006). In too many preschools, being a perfectly normal loud, active boy just isn't acceptable (Tyre, 2008).

> One boy had been doing really well in pre-K. However, when I observed him in Kindergarten, he was wild and off-task much of the time, but I think he was just bored. The teacher did not respond effectively to stimulate and engage him. Instead of finding a challenge that would interest him, she did the opposite and denied him opportunities. (Barbarin & Crawford, 2006, p. 81)

In one study, teachers said that boys were "difficult and take up more than their share of room in the classroom" (Shaffer & Gordon, 2000). The result is that, in many cases, boys are nurtured less and disciplined more (King & Gartrell, 2004).

SOCIAL-EMOTIONAL DEVELOPMENT

The national study conducted by Gilliam mentioned earlier, attesting to the high expulsion rate of boys from preschool, is a clear indication that inadequate attention is being paid to critical social-emotional development. In many cases, teachers and daycare providers are not sufficiently prepared in child development to help boys learn the skills they need to become successful members of the school community—skills such as impulse control, anger control, and the ability to make friends. In the words of Comer, the lack of attention paid to social-emotional development in schools or in learning is the "critical missing link in school reform" (Comer, 2005).

The stigmatization of African American boys begins in preschool and continues through the grades. Classmates quickly pick up on the message that the "bad" boys are African American (Barbarin & Crawford, 2006).

Relational teaching is a key factor in the development of social-emotional skills. Research has shown how the relational life of a classroom shapes social-emotional development and learning, particularly for boys. In one study, a group of teachers, pre-K through high school, met monthly for 1 year to describe individual boys in their classes using the Descriptive Review process. In Descriptive Review, teachers take the time to look at something deeply using descriptive rather than evaluative language. In this particular case, the research focused on the teachers' relationship with boys and how the notions of gender shaped those relationships. At the end of the study, teachers reported an overall shift in their relationship with the observed students; their understanding of boys had changed (Raider-Roth, 2003).

Chu (2000) has studied the centrality of relationships from the young boy's point of view. She notes that boys are capable and desirous of relational attachments but learn early on how to mask them or fit them around stereotypical expectations. In her ethnographic studies of boys, she found evidence that relational capabilities detected at infancy carry through early childhood and into adolescence. She examined boys' experiences of gender socialization and explored how boys negotiate their senses of self, behaviors, and relationships in light of cultural constructions of masculinity. She concludes that boys learn to anticipate how others will respond to them and accordingly modify their self-expression and styles of relating.

Relationships with caring adults in the school as well as in the home are essential to the development of a child's positive sense of self, trust in

Boys feel angry, anxious, sad, and restricted by expectations that they adhere to a rigid set of behaviors that has become known as the "boy code" (Pollack, 1998; Kindlon & Thompson, 1999).

others, and the ability to successfully negotiate social situations through-out life (Raider-Roth, 2005). There is a growing body of research indicating that the social-emotional climate of the early childhood classroom is sa-lient to children's academic performance in later grades. It is increasingly evident that a sense of self-worth and positive, supportive, social-emotional relationships with teachers are central to academic success (Pianta, Cox, & Snow, 2007).

BOYS AND LITERACY

In the 1990s, the growing literacy gap between girls and boys commanded attention. Researchers noted that in kindergarten, girls begin outperform-ing boys in reading by 0.9 points, but by the spring the difference has nearly doubled. The gap continues to grow as boys move from elementary school to middle school and high school. By 12th grade, boys score 16 points lower in reading and 24 points lower in writing than girls (U.S. Department of Education, 2004), and three-fourths of this gap has opened by fourth grade (Newkirk, 2003).

Although the widening literacy gap between boys and girls has re-ceived much attention in both the popular and educational press, it is not the case that boys are "naturally" bad readers, any more than girls are "naturally" bad in science and math. It may be true that some boys start a little behind girls in language, but then this small difference gets amplified by messages that boys often get about the importance (or lack thereof) of reading (Tyre, 2008).

The gender gap in literacy may very well be the result of socialization that begins early and eventually provides different opportunities for boys and girls to develop their abilities. A research study of story-reading to preschool children found that mothers of boys and girls reported similar amounts of reading time when their children were in preschool. However, in the way that they read to their sons and daughters, mothers conveyed

Boys score 16 points lower in reading and 24 points lower in writing than girls (U.S. Department of Education, 2004). Three-fourths of this gap has opened up by grade four (Newkirk, 2003).

a subtle message that reading was for girls and rough-and-tumble play was for boys (Porche, Ross, & Snow, 2004). Mothers tended to request more information about and talk more about books when interacting with their daughters, and their conversations included more praise and encouragement.

ACTIVE LEARNING THROUGH PLAY

Two trends are happening simultaneously in the field of early childhood education: One is known as the "push-down" curriculum, basically bringing pencil-and-paper tasks into preschool; the other is a commitment to remain true to active learning through play as the core early childhood curriculum. Cutting down on play activities for structured learning sessions can be stressful for children whose pent-up energy creates tension for themselves and those around them. Reducing recess and free play, which some programs have done in the name of "learning," is counterproductive for active young children, girls and boys alike (Miller & Almon, 2009).

Pellegrini looked at the effects of recess on elementary school children. He found that successful peer interaction at recess was an excellent predictor of success on standardized tests. He reports that when children, especially boys, establish competence in the schoolyard, they do better in school (Pellegrini & Bohn study, as cited in Tyre, 2008). As Ginsburg (2007) states in a recent article in the journal of the American Academy of Pediatrics, "Reduced time for physical activity may be contributing to the discordant academic ability between boys and girls, because schools that promote sedentary styles of learning become a more difficult environment for boys to navigate successfully." (p. 184)

SCHOOL, FAMILY, AND COMMUNITY PARTNERSHIPS

Home, school, and community need to work in partnership with one another to provide an environment in which young boys and girls can realize their social-emotional, cognitive, and physical potential. For boys, the most potent factors in early development are the emotional support, caring, and consistent expectations provided at home, at school, and in the community (Benard, 2004). A nurturing father can help his son develop a socially accepted moral system (Zaman, 2007). Nurturing male teachers can model that physical activity is a natural part of a young child's life and that active learning should be a natural part of the daily curriculum (Gartrell, 2006).

Irvine describes a lack of "cultural synchronization," a mismatch between teachers and children caused by gender, race, class, and language (as cited in Bowman & Moore, 2006). The mismatch also extends to children's families and communities. Differences in class, culture, and language can become major barriers to home/school communication. These differences can also become a source of stress for children who may not be able to navigate two systems simultaneously.

Warm, supportive, and nurturing relationships must form the base of a child's home life and school life. Without this critical element, there can be no "school readiness." It is imperative that families, schools, and communities work together to provide the support that children need to succeed.

OVERRIDING ISSUES

The chapters in this book are devoted to a discussion of issues that contribute to the fact that boys are not faring as well as they could be in grades pre-K–3. Several issues, however, cut across all the others and take an enormous toll on boys' social-emotional well-being and school success: the intersection of gender with race, ethnicity, and socioeconomic status; the overrepresentation of boys in special education; and the negative effects of the "push-down" curriculum.

*Intersection of Gender/Race/Ethnicity/Socioeconomic Status.*There is evidence that race, ethnicity, and socioeconomic status combine with gender to make boys of color particularly vulnerable to the consternation of teachers and to poor academic performance (Barbarin & Crawford, 2006; Mead, 2006). It is possible that cultural differences cause the perception on the part of teachers that African American boys are "misbehaving" (Smith, 2002).

Boys of color are most likely to suffer serious, long-term consequences when they are not developmentally ready to invest in academics in the lower elementary grades or perceive that by resisting the authority of a female teacher they are laying legitimate claim to their male prerogatives. Teachers' discomfort with boys' noncompliant behavior can easily lead

In 2000–2001, African American boys made up 8.6% of national public school enrollment, but made up 20% of those classified as mentally retarded, 21% of those classified as emotionally disturbed, 22% of those expelled from school, and 23% of those suspended (Smith, 2002).

to premature referrals for special education, prescriptions for medication, school suspensions, and retention in grade. According to a report from the President's Commission on Excellence in Special Education (as cited in Smith, 2003), minority children are much more likely to be placed in the emotional disturbance category because of biased attitudes and a lack of understanding of the cultural context in which a child is raised.

In *The Evidence Suggests Otherwise*, Mead argues that race and class are more salient factors in achievement gaps than gender. She notes, though, that when racial and economic gaps combine with gender achievement gaps in reading, there are groups of boys (poor, African American, and Latino boys, in particular) for whom *crisis* is not too strong a term (Mead, 2006). There is the hope, however, that the presidency of Barack Obama will change the situation for these boys. Boys of color can now see that, despite the stereotypes, they can aspire to heights that were at one time inconceivable. Although this does not erase the challenges of the past, it does mean that the probability for the academic success of African American males increases exponentially (Kafele, 2009).

Special Education. Rather than creating a learning environment that celebrates boys' energy and respects their need for active play, teachers often find it more convenient to ease energetic or, in their minds, troublesome boys out of the regular classroom into special education—or medicate them (Gartrell, 2006).

Boys are prescribed medicine for attention-related disorders at twice the rate of girls. Between 2000 and 2005, the number of boys being medicated grew 48% (Tyre, 2008). Dr. Perri Klass, a noted pediatrician, has reported that boys she has known from the time they are 2 hours old and seen grow into healthy, active toddlers, reach preschool and are regarded as hyperactive, not able to pay attention, and needing medication (Klass, 2009).

> Boys make up two-thirds of students in special education—including 80% of those diagnosed with emotional disturbances or autism—and boys are two and a half times as likely as girls to be diagnosed with attention deficit hyperactivity disorder (ADHD) (U.S. Department of Education, 2003).

For well over 30 years, the fact that boys are vastly overrepresented in special education has been an issue of concern. Although there are children for whom special education is beneficial, the truth is that one way schools deal with "problem" boys is to refer them to special education. The statistics bear this out: Boys comprise two-thirds of the special education population, are two and a half times as likely as girls to be diagnosed with ADHD, are four times as likely as girls to be referred to a school psychologist, and comprise 80% of children who are diagnosed with emotional disturbance or autism (Conference on Minorities in Special Education, 2001; USDOE, 2003; Kindlon & Thompson, 1999). A disproportionate number of these boys are African American and Latino. In 2000–2001, African American boys made up 8.6% of national public school enrollment, but 20% of those classified as mentally retarded, 21% of those classified as emotionally disturbed, 22% of those expelled from school, and 23% of those suspended (Smith, 2002).

The "Push-Down" Curriculum. The "push-down" curriculum is driven by a national climate of high-stakes testing and a federal mandate to have every child become fluent in reading by the end of third grade, a worthy goal with, in too many instances, a developmentally inappropriate method of achievement. Preschool and kindergarten children doing seat work, filling out worksheets, or repeating consonant and vowel sounds without a context will not make fluent readers who comprehend the meaning of words or ever enjoy reading. For boys, seat work and other formal aspects of the school day are especially stressful, given that they often enter school at an earlier stage of maturity than girls—sometimes with a lag of 12–18 months.

The push-down curriculum, which greatly limits free-play periods and often eliminates recess in the interest of "work time," exacts the greatest toll on boys of color from low-income families. Marcon (as cited in

Tyre, 2008) followed poor African American children from three different preschools: one that was academically focused, another that favored child-initiated activities, and one that was a combination. By fourth grade, children who attended academically focused preschools earned significantly lower grades and behaved worse than children from the other two preschools. Boys who were best able to keep pace with girls had attended the child-initiated schools. The boys who fell furthest behind were ones who had attended academic preschools.

The tension between teacher-directed instruction and child-initiated, experiential learning is not new. The issue has been debated since at least the 1950s, and has its roots in the Sputnik era, when the Soviets beat the United States into space, and the United States was concerned that our education system wasn't keeping up. For example, in the 1970s, the High Scope model, which exemplified a child-initiated and teacher-facilitated play approach, was pitched against the Bereiter-Engelmann model, which promoted a behavioral approach featuring scripted, direct instruction lessons delivered by the teacher to small groups of children. Both High Scope and Bereiter-Engelmann were sincere in trying to improve school success for poor children who were considered at high risk. However, a longitudinal study carried out by the High Scope Foundation showed that children who attended a play-based nursery school or the High Scope preschool had half the rate of delinquency at age 15, and, at age 23, showed statistically significant advantages over the direct instruction group. Compared to the direct instruction group, the High Scope and nursery school group had fewer arrests and fewer years of special education for emotional impairment. Knowing that the population mostly referred to special education are African American and Latino boys from low-income families, it can be inferred from the High Scope study that direct instruction programs do not serve the needs of these children. The research also documented that children who attended the High Scope or a nursery school program completed a higher level of schooling and had more stable family relationships as adults (Schweinhart & Weikart, 1997).

Boys represent 70% of school suspensions, with a disproportionate number of minority males in urban schools represented in this figure (Ferguson, 2000).

Despite the irrefutable evidence of the High Scope research, since the year 2000, there has been a repeat trend toward early academics and direct instruction in preschool and kindergarten. As stated earlier, this trend is driven by a desire to close the achievement gap. However, pushing early academics so children can perform well on tests that begin in fourth grade is not the road to success for many boys.

Fortunately, the pendulum seems to be swinging back. Leaders in the field of early childhood education are advocating a return to a developmentally appropriate approach that includes ample time for play, both child-initiated and teacher-guided, and to a learning environment that focuses on social-emotional development. The turn-around needs to happen soon. For boys, developmentally inappropriate curriculum can lead to a sense of failure that begins in preschool and follows them throughout their school career.

CONCLUSION

In *The Trouble with Boys*, Tyre (2008) discusses three myths about boys and school that she believes are the roadblocks to change. Myth #1: For boys, school achievement doesn't matter. Myth #2: Boys who struggle early on eventually will catch up. Myth #3: Schools have always done it this way, so it's the way it's supposed to be (pp. 13–14).

The positive side of the coin is that children can show resilience against all odds. The research on resiliency encourages a strength-based perspective on development and education. The guiding principle of resiliency is the presumption of an individual's innate capacity for strengths (Benard, 2004). For example, girls and boys have an innate capacity to be assertive and to be nurturing. Resilience for boys is correlated with family and school environments that encourage emotional expressiveness, beginning in early childhood.

In September 2006, *Educational Leadership*, the journal of the Association for Supervision and Curriculum Development, devoted an entire issue to the topic of "Teaching to Student Strengths." Article after article urged teachers to understand that every child has some strengths that can foster learning, to look for the positive qualities in each child and build on them, to recognize rather than neglect children's strong points, and, always, to challenge deficit thinking about students within themselves and their colleagues (Scherer, 2006).

As teachers enter the profession they come face-to-face with the realities of high-stakes testing and mandated curriculum. Taking time to know children as people as well as learners is essential. Trying to remember that teaching is about relationships is a true challenge, especially for a new teacher. And it is particularly challenging when it comes to relationships between teachers and boys.

The consequences of turning boys off to education at an early age are severe and long-term, but the opposite is also true. Turning boys on to education can reverse the current trend that places all boys, but especially African American and Latino boys, at risk of failure.

If teachers have the skills, strategies, and support systems to nurture resilience, build on children's strengths, and understand that teaching is about relationships, then all children can achieve. These factors are essential in terms of boys' development and school success. The challenge is to:

- Create learning environments where social-emotional development has the highest priority;
- Refuse to view any child from a deficit model;
- Understand that every child has strengths to build on, hidden though they may be;
- Look for cultural connections, not disconnections, with families and communities;
- Counteract prevailing stereotypes about masculinity.

FOR FURTHER REFLECTION

- What are some ways to help teachers re-examine their attitudes and expectations about boys?
- Why is it important to view boys' energy as a valuable asset to active learning?
- What are some strategies for carving out time and space in the school day for learning through play?

KEY READINGS

Barbarin, O., & Crawford, G. (2006). Reducing the stigmatization of African American males. *Young Children*, 61(6), 79–86.

This article reports on a random study conducted in more than 100 pre-K and kindergarten classrooms that revealed that African American boys were stigmatized as "bad boys" and, once labeled, the stigmatization followed the boys from grade to grade.

Garbarino, J. (1999). *Lost boys: Why our sons turn violent and how we can save them.* New York: The Free Press.

> *Written to help families understand male anger and prevent violence in their sons, the case studies in this book provide valuable insights for teachers. Garbarino points to the value of positive male role models from the community in keeping boys on a path to an education and career rather than the streets.*

Gilliam, W. S. (2005). *Prekindergartners left behind: Expulsion rates in state prekindergarten programs.* Foundation for Child Development, Policy Brief, Series No. 3, May 2005.

> *This large, national study documented that expulsions from preschool occur three times more often than the national K–12 expulsion rate, that boys are five times more likely to be expelled than girls, and that African American boys are three times more likely to be expelled than White children.*

King, M., with Gartrell, D. (2004). Guidance with boys in early childhood classrooms. In D. Gartell (Ed.), *The power of guidance: Teaching social-emotional skills in early childhood classrooms* (pp. 106–24). Clifton Park, NY: Delmar/Thompson Learning and NAEYC.

> *This chapter makes the point that if early childhood education were made more developmentally appropriate for all children, boys and girls alike would benefit. Through the device of a "composite" case study, the authors revisit every aspect of the classroom—scheduling, room arrangement, meeting time, and indoor/outdoor curriculum—with the goal of making the classroom more responsive to boys' needs.*

Scherer, M. (Ed.). (2006). Teaching to student strengths. *Educational Leadership, 64* (1).

> *The entire issue of the magazine is devoted to looking at children from a perspective of their strengths rather than a deficit model. Examples of articles include "Relationships Matter," "The Power of Positive Identity," and "Challenging Deficit Thinking."*

Tyre, P. (2008). *The trouble with boys: A surprising report card on our sons, their problems at school, and what parents and educators must do.* New York: Crown Publishers.

> *The author, through hundred of interviews conducted with parents, teachers, experts in the field, and boys, looks at how our educational system is failing boys, leading to their disengagement from school. Tyre takes on high-stress academics beginning in preschool, the reduction and/or banning of recess, and the skewed approach to brain research.*

CHAPTER 2

Boys Are Not the Problem

Reflecting About Boys and Masculinity

John is 7 years old and is in the second grade. His parents are professionals, and he is an only child. There is a rich social studies and science curriculum in his classroom, with many opportunities for children to make choices based on their own interests. When given the opportunity, John demonstrates a deep interest in the natural world. For example, during outdoor recess, his eyes are often turned upward as he watches birds fly by. On a recent trip to the local park, he accurately called out the names of birds that he saw (sparrow, cardinal, blue jay). When outdoors, John is often engaged in solitary observations that he enjoys reporting to the teacher. He has rarely been observed engaging in outdoor play activities with his peers.

In the classroom, John often approaches the teacher with questions about the work that he is doing and tries to engage the teacher in extended conversations. However, he does not take the same initiative with his peers, and they do not take the initiative to recruit him when there are opportunities to engage in open-ended activities of their choosing.

In a recent parent conference, the teacher expressed to John's parents her concern about his relationships with other children. She felt he relied too heavily on her and other adults for social interaction and that he should be more involved in more typical, rough-and-tumble play with other boys. She suggested that his parents enroll him in a soccer or softball league. His parents responded that they had indeed suggested this to John, but he was not interested. The teacher said that decisions like this should not rest solely with him.

This anecdote raises a number of questions about sex-role socialization. What makes rough-and-tumble play "typical" for boys? Why is it considered "normal" for a boy to be interested in sports? Is a boy who does not like sports considered "abnormal"? Why shouldn't John be encouraged to explore his interest in the natural world?

SEX-ROLE SOCIALIZATION BEGINS EARLY

Expectations around gender roles begin before a child is born. Parents-to-be are asked, "Is it a boy?" or "Is it a girl?" Thus, the pink and blue gender divide begins, and it is reinforced by baby presents, clothes, toys, bedding—even baby congratulations cards. Cards convey their messages through pink and blue color-coding, and through not-so-subtle stereotyped images. "Boy cards" show boys (usually older than an infant) "in action," playing with balls, sports equipment, cars, and trucks. "Girl cards" typically show inactive girls, immobile in cribs or baskets surrounded by rattles, flowers, and teddy bears. The written messages indicate that boys can be anything, while girls are forever small, precious, little girls (Bridges, 1993).

Very young children learn about how girls and boys are "supposed" to behave through adult responses as well (Andersen & Hysock, 2008; Richardson, 1988; Thorne, 1994; Unger & Crawford, 1992). Studies have shown that parents react differently toward their newborn sons and daughters (Rubin, Provenzano, & Luria, 1974). Shown an infant dressed in girl's clothing and boy's clothing, new parents described the "girl" as tiny, delicate, and precious; the "boy" as big, a bruiser, a future football player. In fact, it was the same infant, only the clothing was different (Fagot, 1978).

In an article entitled "Little Boys Blue: Reexamining the Plight of Young Males," columnist Megan Rosenfeld tells this story:

> A mother takes her five-year-old son to buy a new bike. At the time, his favorite color was pink, so he wanted a pink bike. But the salesman said that pink is a "girl color," and he should use red or blue. The boy still wanted pink, so he got his pink bike. Then other children began to call him "gay." They teased him so much, he put a sign on his bike explaining his choice of color. But this wore on him and now, at age 8, he learned his "lesson." He doesn't let anyone know he likes pink. (Rosenfeld, 1998)

The effects of this sex-role stereotyping has long-term consequences. In 1985, Greenberg wrote, "It is learning the prescribed sex role rather than learning of one's gender identity that often has limiting and damaging effects on subsequent development" (p. 457).

EFFECTS OF THE BOY CODE

What exactly are the limiting and damaging effects for boys? If becoming a boy means becoming tough, then boys may feel at an early age that they have to hide the part of themselves that is more caring or stereotypically feminine (Viadero, 1998). Pollack (1998) has coined the phrase "the boy code" to express the constraints on boys' emotional development and the resulting inner emotional pain that many boys carry around under the façade of being "normal" and "fine." These constraints also have been called "emotional illiteracy" (Kindlon & Thompson, 1999).

Kimmel (2000) has written that "masculinity is the key to understanding boyhood and its current crisis." (p. 7) In order to conform to a societal conception of what it means to be a man, boys have been placed in a "box," an ideal of masculinity that limits their emotional and relational development (Flood, 2000). The consequences of operating outside the "box" are severe. Boys who do so are labeled in ways that leave them feeling isolated and shamed.

For a recent project, called Raising and Educating Healthy Boys (see Acknowledgments), the authors of this book conducted a series of focus groups with pre-K–3 teachers and parents. During the focus groups, each adult was asked to fill in two boxes:

Box 1: What does it mean to be male in our society?
Box 2: What happens to boys who don't fit into Box 1?

Results of the first question showed that both groups see that boys are expected to be competent, do well in school and at work, be leaders in the family, and be physically powerful. Results of the second question revealed real concern from both parents and teachers for boys who don't fit in. Both groups saw that boys were at psychological risk if they didn't fit in, and they were well aware of the pain and suffering that could result as a consequence—for example, antisocial behavior, hardships and pressures, and impact on sexuality and gender identity.

The focus groups point to a "Damned if you do; damned if you don't" situation for boys. There are high expectations for boys to be instrumentally competent and physically powerful—to demonstrate competence in every area of their lives, including school and sports as children, and in the family and workplace as adults (Gropper, 2004). Although a sense of instrumental competence is a desirable goal, it is a tall order for young boys to be good at everything deemed "masculine." For example, many young boys may not have the physical coordination to be outstanding athletes; they may not be social leaders; they may not yet—or ever—have the skills to be academic stars. Because a sense of competence is a compelling need, in the short run, preschool and kindergarten boys may strive for feelings of competence by assuming what they perceive to be their "male prerogatives"—assertive voices, play fighting and even real fighting, and resistance to authority, particularly when the authority figure is a female teacher. As they move into the elementary grades, should they not develop competency in other, more school-acceptable realms, they run the risk of "getting stuck" in stereotypic boy behavior that is likely to provoke increasing social disapproval and other negative consequences as they move into the elementary grades. The playful roughhousing of early childhood can later spiral into a reputation as the class troublemaker, leading to all the risks that are delineated in this chapter. But the ostensible demands to be masculine may also lead to feelings of social isolation and role confusion for boys who do not behave in stereotypic male ways.

Whether it's the fear of being called a "wuss" or a "sissy," or the threat of being identified as feminine, boys of all ages are keenly aware of the strict behavioral boundaries set by the masculine ideal and the high price that is exacted from them for playing "out of bounds." In boys, the development of empathy and the ability to express it are acutely limited by such homophobic boundaries. Homophobia is broader than the fear of homosexuality; it is a prohibition so profound that it extends to the expression of any emotion or feeling, much less a behavior or action, considered to be feminine (Kimmel, 2000).

BRAIN RESEARCH AND GENDER

A baby is born as a biological boy or girl. But very early on, the wider society begins to limit the child, telling him or her what rules to follow because he is a boy or she is a girl. This "invented" set of rules differs across cultures, changes over time, and serves to teach and prescribe what a boy or girl should be (Katz, 1999).

Young children's developing gender identities and perceptions about gender roles are actively constructed based in large part on social experience (MacNaughton, 2000). In their effort to accurately apply gender labels to themselves and others, very young children initially rely on perceptual cues such as hairstyle, dress, and activities that are associated with one gender or the other. It is not until sometime between 5 and 7 years of

While traveling home from work on a commuter train, one of the authors of this book was avidly reading *The Trouble With Boys* by Peg Tyre. A woman sitting next to her started a conversation by saying, "I can't help but noticing the book you are reading." The woman went on to explain that her second-grade son was being called disruptive and troublesome by his teacher. The woman had been called to school on several occasions and was being pressured to have her son evaluated and put on medication. In her view, her son was a perfectly fine, active child who was not in need of psychological evaluation or medication. She did say that the demands for sitting still and lack of physical activity made school difficult for him, and he was beginning to be upset by being told that he was not behaving well. The author advised this mother to share Peg Tyre's book with the principal and teacher and, if necessary, try to get her son into another second-grade classroom.

age that they attain the cognitive capacity to understand that gender is anatomically defined and relatively constant (Kohlberg, 1966). Once they attain this understanding, children are freer to think more flexibly about gender roles, but it is then that limitations are set by societally imposed and internalized stereotypic behaviors and interests.

Fueling this situation is the misuse of current research on the differences between male and female brains (Gurian, Henley, & Trueman, 2001). Although research on brain-based learning has been conducted since the 1950s, and can inform educators about ways to make learning more effective for all students, teachers must be cautious about how it is put to use in classrooms. There's a trend in the educational world to take a little brain-based science and run with it, but there is a danger that if the research is understood and interpreted only at a superficial level, it can be taken too far. For example, in the current use of brain research, too often there is an assumption of a clear link between brain anatomy on the one hand and learning behaviors and academic achievement on the other (Newkirk, 2005). Tyre (2008) tells of this exchange with a principal who was basing the following observation on "hard evidence" from brain scans: "Our kindergarten girls like to sit on the rug and talk in the morning. Because of their oxytocin levels, they want to bond. But boys, because of their testosterone, like to run around. They just do. It's their biology." (p. 180).

The concern is that what brain researchers posit as innate differences in the abilities of males and females could, in the long run, reinforce old gender stereotypes (Tyre, 2008). Arguments in the line of "women are from Venus" and "men are from Mars" ignore the wide variation among individuals of the same sex and the fact that there are far more similarities than differences between genders (Mead, 2006; Hyde, 2005).

STRATEGIES

In 1985, in an influential chapter on educational equity in early childhood environments, Dr. Selma Greenberg suggested classroom strategies that are strikingly relevant today. Many of the following suggestions are based on her advice.

Intentionally provide boys with opportunities that encourage nurturing and a sense of responsibility for others. Taking care of a class pet or tending to growing plants are critical experiences that will help boys express emotions that, because of the "strong silent" male stereotype, they often keep to themselves. Dramatic play offers myriad opportunities for boys to engage in caregiving activities that they may not choose on their own, such as a "hospital" where boys can be nurses or doctors, or a "nursery" where they can take care of babies. Water play areas also can be set up to help boys take on nurturing roles, such as bathing and then feeding male doll babies. Other dramatic play scenarios such as a "store" or "space station" may also attract boys.

Provide opportunities for boys to connect with a variety of male role models that provide exposure to a broad range of possibilities—from sports figures to technology experts to nurturing professionals. Gartrell (2006) has noted that there is a need for males in the early childhood classroom who naturally "speak the language of boys." Male teachers can bring a comfort with physical activity into the classroom, and they can model (for teachers as well as children) that active learning should be a natural part of the daily curriculum. Male relatives can be invited into the classroom as role models. For example, a father, grandfather, uncle, or older brother can lead or help with a cooking or photography activity.

Create a buddy system with older boys in the school. Younger children look up to older students and love being around them. It is also beneficial for the older students to see how much the younger ones are learning as they play. Older boys can read to a group of younger boys, organize a game during recess, or talk about their interests during a class meeting.

Have a male role model place himself in areas that boys may not frequent. Research conducted some years ago about how to engage girls in block building showed that the teacher (or other adult) in the block area works like a magnet (Serbin, Conner, & Citron, 1978). This strategy can work for boys as well, by having an older student or visitor seat himself in the kitchen area or at the table where small-motor materials are set out.

Ask boys to interview their male relatives about how they helped out at home when they were children. Boys in grades 1–3 can write and use a simple questionnaire to gather information. In earlier grades, male relatives can visit the classroom to answer the questions verbally.

Provide books about adult males and boys who don't fit the "masculine" stereotype but are true to themselves and successful in other ways. Books about men involved in the caring professions, such as male nurses or teachers, can help boys expand their ideas of what is acceptable for them. On a trip to the school library, the librarian or an older student can read a book such as *Oliver Button Is a Sissy* by De Paola or *Frederick* by Lionni and lead a discussion. Many publishers put out series of books that address feelings and issues. (See the Appendix C section for suggestions.)

Create a boys' reading club led by older boys to engage boys in reading for pleasure. For first- through third-graders, a reading club could be a lunchtime activity—in one school, they called it "chat 'n' chew." For preschoolers, it can be another storytime, with an older boy as the storyteller. Some coaching on how to tell stories effectively would be useful.

CONCLUSION

Gender stereotypes—whether for boys or girls—interfere with children's learning. They begin early, and they put in place restrictive ideas about masculinity and femininity that limit children's cognitive, social, and emotional development. Teachers need to address issues of sex-role stereotyping beginning in early childhood, and they need to create learning environments so that boys are not lost to the community of learning (Koch & Irby, 2002).

FOR FURTHER REFLECTION

- What role do gender stereotypes about masculinity play in boys' social, emotional, and academic development?
- How do gender stereotypes relate to the expectations and practices of teachers?
- What words and ideas are associated with the word *boy*—are they positive or negative?
- Are boys expected to be strong and competent? What happens to boys who do not meet these expectations?
- How does the misuse of current brain research reinforce sex-role stereotypes?

KEY READINGS

Ferguson, A. (2000). *Bad boys: Public school in the making of black masculinity.* Ann Arbor: University of Michigan Press.

> *Based on 3 years of participant observation research at an elementary school,* Bad Boys *offers an account of daily interactions between teachers and students to understand why African American males are disproportionately getting in trouble and being suspended from school.*

Hull, G., Kenney, N. L., Marple, S., & Forman-Schneider, A. (2006). Many versions of masculine: An exploration of boys' identity formation through digital storytelling in an afterschool program. *Afterschool Matters.* Occasional Paper Series #6. Spring 2006.

> *This paper reports on research about boys and masculinity and features case studies of nine urban boys of color who participated in an afterschool program where they learned to create digital multimedia texts. The study reveals that, through movies, narration, photographs and music, these children demonstrated many versions of their masculine selves in contrast to the more one-dimensional portraits often portrayed in popular literature.*

Kindlon, D., & Thompson, M. (1999). *Raising Cain: Protecting the emotional life of boys.* New York: Ballantine Books.

> *The authors share insights on boys' emotional development from birth through college and argue that boys desperately need a new standard of "emotional literacy." They discuss how our culture's dominant masculine stereotypes shortchange boys and lead them toward emotional isolation. They also challenge the ways in which, in their view, traditional school environments put boys at a disadvantage.*

Pollack, W. (1998). *Real boys: Rescuing our sons from the myths of boyhood.* New York: Random House.

> *Harvard Medical School psychiatry professor William Pollack describes what he terms "the Boy Code"—society's image of boys as tough, cool, and rambunctious. These stereotypes, he argues, thwart creativity and originality in boys. He advises caregivers on how to help boys develop empathy and explore their sensitive sides.*

CHAPTER 3

Social-Emotional Development

A Critical Factor for School Success

Like most parents, the Johnsons wanted only the best for their 5-year-old son, Anthony. In their Midwest school district, grades K–3 were housed in separate buildings and parents could choose between two different types of programs. One school offered an academic approach beginning in kindergarten and the other one was more traditional early childhood, at least in kindergarten. After visiting both schools, the Johnsons chose the more academic program. Even though Anthony had only just turned 5, they thought that the academic program would give their boy a "head start." The Johnsons reasoned that since Anthony had been in a preschool program when he was 4, he didn't need more of "that play stuff."

Anthony didn't thrive in the academically oriented kindergarten. He showed signs of stress and often cried in the morning, saying he didn't want to go to school. At a parent conference in the fall, the teacher said that it was difficult for Anthony to pay attention during work time and he often cried in frustration when he couldn't finish a worksheet. She suggested a talk with the school psychologist. The Johnsons left the conference worried about their bright little boy, and they made an appointment to speak with the psychologist.

Dr. Greene, the psychologist, had looked over Anthony's records in preparation for the meeting. He helped the Johnsons see that, for Anthony, a "head start" was a program that was a better fit with his developmental level. Dr. Greene said that, in his opinion, the program with less focus on academics would allow Anthony, who was one of the youngest children in his class, time and space to develop social-emotional skills that would serve him well over the long term. He suggested a midyear move to the other K–3 school. It was a hard choice for the Johnsons to make, but they didn't want their boy to have school problems.

During morning meeting on the first day in his new kindergarten, the children sang a welcome song to Anthony. The teacher made special time in the week to find out about the things Anthony liked to do, and helped him to feel that he belonged. Within a couple of weeks, Anthony was bubbling about school, talking about new friends, and using his teacher's favorite expressions at home. Somewhat reluctantly, the Johnsons had to agree that the program that paid attention to Anthony's social-emotional needs really was the "head start" he needed.

REAL "SCHOOL READINESS"

Like Anthony's well-intentioned but misguided parents, whole school systems have veered off course by focusing on early academics at the expense of social-emotional development in the name of "school readiness." Social-emotional competence, however, is at the core of early childhood education, and is a key factor in boys' success in school. It is the most important skill young children need to acquire. In the rush to "push down" academics into the early childhood years, attention to the development of this vital skill has too often been sidelined, to the detriment of all children, but especially boys.

The Collaborative for Academic, Social, and Emotional Learning (CASEL) has defined social-emotional skill as the ability to calm oneself when angry, initiate friendships, resolve conflicts respectfully, make ethical and safe choices, and contribute constructively to the community (Collaborative for Academic, Social, and Emotional Learning, 2007; Miller & Almon, 2009). Goleman (1995), a cofounder of CASEL and known worldwide for his work on emotional intelligence, believes that social-emotional skills such as self-awareness, self-discipline, persistence, and empathy are as vital as cognitive skills measured by IQ and achievement tests. A meta-analysis of 200 research studies conducted by CASEL gives further weight to the importance of social-emotional learning in early childhood. Studies show that children who attend programs that focus on social-emotional development do better academically, have higher rates of attendance, and are safer in school (Epstein, 2009). Many other early childhood organizations, such as NAEYC, have guidelines for social-emotional learning written into their policies (Copple & Bredekamp, 2009).

RELATIONAL TEACHING AND SOCIAL-EMOTIONAL DEVELOPMENT

In order to create a learning environment where every child feels valued, teachers must take the time and effort to reach each child on a relational level. Raider-Roth (2005) speaks about the importance of trust in human relationships and defines four central features of a "trustworthy teaching-learning relationship"—the teacher's capacity to be connected to her students, the teacher's genuine interest in nurturing students' own ideas, collaborative study on the part of teacher and students, and an environment in which trust can prevail. One of Raider-Roth's students, an experienced kindergarten teacher, expressed her frustration about the push for early academics during a class on the Relational Context of Teaching and Learning. She stated, "I'm thinking, in the light of increasing standards-based work in the classroom and the need to justify every moment spent in the classroom with children, about how 'relationship' is being trivialized, marginalized" (p. 167).

Research shows that teachers in grades K–5 who provide high levels of instructional and *emotional* (emphasis added) support close the achievement gap for at-risk children (Pianta, Cox, & Snow, 2007). Many preschool and early primary grade teachers are aware that what they are mandated to do is not developmentally appropriate and lament the fact that they no longer have time for the relational aspects of teaching. It is a paradox—instead of a focus on social-emotional development and an active-learning, experiential approach that was the heart and soul of early childhood education filtering up through the grades, the more didactic, structured way of teaching typical in the mid-elementary grades has filtered downward. It is clear that when pre-kindergarten, kindergarten, and primary grade children have warm, caring relationships with their teachers, these relationships foster development and learning (Pianta, Hamre, & Stuhlman, as cited in Copple & Bredekamp, 2009).

One of this book's authors has observed that teachers are under pressure in terms of academics being pushed down into kindergarten. In some kindergarten classrooms, children are now expected to read and write for more than 1 hour a day, and recess is being eliminated in many places. In the current climate, many teachers feel they cannot adequately attend to social-emotional issues.

THE CONSEQUENCES OF NONRELATIONAL TEACHING

Unfortunately, in many schools, this lack of relational teaching has a detrimental effect on the early schooling experience of too many boys. Raider-Roth's principles of trust that enable a child to thrive in school are a far cry from the teacher who stigmatizes a young boy as "bad," the teacher who recommends expelling a 4-year-old boy, or a teacher who deprives a child of recess because he is unable to sit still during a "lesson."

The consequences of not addressing boys' social-emotional needs in early childhood can be severe and long-lasting. As discussed in Chapter 1, a national study conducted by Gilliam (2005) revealed that boys are being expelled from preschool at alarming rates, and the vast majority of the children who are expelled are African American boys. In interviews with teachers, Gilliam found many who were willing to admit that they were unable to handle overactive boys or what they considered to be behavioral problems. When Gilliam asked teachers if they had expelled a child from their classroom for behavioral problems in the last 12 months, one in 10 teachers replied that they had. Gilliam wrote that lack of teacher preparation and support services such as school-based social workers and psychologists were at the root of these expulsions.

In the study conducted by Barbarin and Crawford (2006), two-person teams of trained observers visited more than 100 randomly selected pre-K through kindergarten classrooms and recorded the instructional and emotional climate of each classroom. The researchers found that African American boys were stigmatized as "bad boys," made to sit in isolation next to the teacher's desk, and often shunned by other children. In the words of one observer, "I observed it over and over again. And it wasn't just that it was only boys, it was always, always, Black Boys" (p. 80). What the observers found was so disturbing to them that they brought their findings to the attention of the supervisors of the study even before the research was completed.

Once a child is labeled as a troublemaker, the label is passed on from teacher to teacher and the process of disengagement from school is under way. Why would any child want to stay in a place where he is made to feel shamed, isolated, and not liked? Expelling a boy from preschool or stigmatizing him as "bad" from the time he enters school is the beginning of the achievement gap and the high school dropout rate that limits the potential of far too many children and deprives society of a vast pool of human talent.

The work of Gilliam and Barbarin and Crawford sent shockwaves through the field of early childhood education. Their research was a wake-up call that attention must be paid to what is happening to boys in school, and most particularly to African American boys.

RETHINKING
SCHOOL READINESS

Many factors have combined to take a heavy toll on the social-emotional development and well-being of boys in school: mandated, teacher-directed curriculum that requires children to "learn" in ways that are not developmentally appropriate; teachers who feel pressured to teach to the test instead of the child; teachers who have not been educated to understand and appreciate the ways of boys; and lack of social and psychological support services that should be in every school. Fortunately, educators are once again advocating making time in the early childhood curriculum for the development of social-emotional competence, and providing guidance and strategies that will enable children to acquire this most valu-

Luis, a very bright boy, was diagnosed with severe learning disabilities that made school difficult for him. He never did well and carried a sense of failure around as a chip on his shoulder. He was, however, a handsome and charismatic child. Finally, when Luis entered high school, one teacher took him under wing. He let Luis know that he had two paths he could follow: one to the streets and no future, and one to success, which would require buckling down and overcoming his learning difficulties. Because his teacher sought him out, confronted him, conveyed belief in his ability to succeed, and provided support for his efforts, Luis took the path to success. He graduated college with a degree in mathematics, and became a businessman and a sought-after motivational speaker to show other children with disabilities that they can aspire to and fulfill their dreams.

able "school readiness" tool. In fact, a longitudinal study conducted by Hawkins (1999) showed that students who received intervention strategies to help with their social development in grades 1–6 had reduced rates of violence and use of alcohol, were more likely to complete high school, were above the median in socioeconomic status and education by ages 24 and 27, and had fewer mental health and sexual health problems. The differences begin to show up in the teen years, which, in many cases, is a particularly stressful period. The Hawkins study makes a clear case for the positive results of addressing social-emotional development beginning in preschool and throughout the elementary grades.

STRATEGIES

Intentional strategies for strengthening boys' social-emotional competency can be incorporated into the daily life of the classroom, even one with a mandated academic curriculum. Here are some ideas that worked for teachers in the field.

Make careful observations at the beginning of the school year to define strengths in each boy and use them as a wedge to develop additional strengths (see Chapter 7 for guidelines). For example, if a boy likes playing a particular game, ask him to share his knowledge with the class. Perhaps he can teach some other children to play. Talk about how practice helps him improve his game, and help him see the analogy with practicing reading or writing. Use his interest to put him in a leadership role in the classroom or at recess.

Create a climate of trust by letting each boy know that he is a valued member of the class. Be mindful that boys' interests are often overlooked in early childhood classrooms. Find one special interest of each boy, and carve out a brief time during the school day to talk about it one-on-one. If it is something the whole class would enjoy, ask the boy to share his interest and then build curriculum around it—for example, write a class story about the topic, take books on the topic out of the library, and/or invite someone with expertise in the area to visit the classroom.

Develop a success plan for a boy who is having a difficult time. Together, set one reasonable behavioral goal at a time, and celebrate when he is able to accomplish the goal. The celebration can be small—a high five, a chart of high fives, a chance to lead the line or at a game. Keep building on goal accomplishment throughout the school year, building the child's self-confidence and ability to exert self-control.

Choose books that address a range of emotions with boys as protagonists. Read the books during storytime or with small groups of children, and use them as a catalyst for discussions about feelings. Follow up with puppet or role-plays created by the children that address the feelings in the book. Be especially sensitive to the fact that boys often have a difficult time expressing a range of emotions, and choose books that help free them up. Be mindful that it may take several readings and discussions before boys are ready to participate (see Appendix C for suggestions).

Create "stop action" stories about social-emotional issues that arise in the classroom. Use puppets to outline a situation, and have children come up with possible solutions. Sum up the activity by writing down some positive strategies that could be helpful in real life. Boys in second and third grade might like to create storyboards as a first step toward a graphic book.

CONCLUSION

School readiness is about entering the primary grades with a sense of trust in one's teachers and other adults in the school community. It is about feeling respected, competent, and eager to learn new things. It's about bounding into the classroom full of energy, and knowing that there are positive ways to channel that energy into learning, with a teacher's approval. This confident approach to school comes from relational teaching and attention to the components of social-emotional learning stated at the beginning of this chapter. For boys, and most particularly for boys who are considered at-risk, positive social-emotional development is the most essential skill that preschool and early primary education can provide.

FOR FURTHER REFLECTION

- How can one learn to focus on the positive rather than the negative traits of a boy who causes disturbances in the classroom?
- What professional literature will provide better understanding and strategies for developing boys' social-emotional needs?

- What are the sources for help in working with a child who displays difficult behavior in the classroom?
- Can the classroom arrangement and daily schedule and room arrangement be adjusted to work better for boys?

KEY READINGS

Bowman, B., & Moore, E. (Eds.). (2006). *School readiness and social-emotional development: Perspectives on cultural diversity.* Washington, DC: The National Black Child Development Institute.

> *This book, written by a group of early childhood experts, provides insight on how to achieve positive social-emotional development for African American, Latino, and other children entering school from culturally diverse, low-income families.*

Copple, C., & Bredekamp, S. (Eds.). (2009, 3rd ed.). *Developmentally appropriate practice.* Washington, DC: National Association for the Education of Young Children.

> *This is an essential guide to principles of high-quality education for children ages birth through 8. The 2009 edition issued by NAEYC, the leading national early childhood professional organization, is infused throughout with practical ideas for scaffolding knowledge in developmentally appropriate ways, and building social-emotional skills in the current educational climate.*

Epstein, A. S. (2009). *Me, you, us: Social-emotional learning in preschool.* Ypsilanti, MI: High/Scope Press.

> *This book offers a highly practical approach to addressing the whole range of social-emotional learning, including self-identity, empathy, competence, and community within the school, the home, and the larger community. Summaries of strategies at the end of each chapter are a useful reference tool.*

Raider-Roth, M. B. (2005). *Trusting what you know: The high stakes of relational teaching.* San Francisco: Jossey-Bass.

> *Raider-Roth stresses that vital relationships form the foundations for learning. Although written about a group of sixth graders, the lessons about the importance of teacher-child relationships as the backbone of social-emotional growth are universally applicable.*

CHAPTER 4

Boys and Literacy

Fostering and Sustaining Literacy Development

As a young child, Carlos was late to talk and struggled with the mechanics of learning to read. Intervention began in first grade and continued through fifth grade. An evaluation by a school psychologist indicated that although he ". . . earned scores above grade level in reading comprehension (he was) below in accuracy and speed . . . an indication that the mechanics of reading still thwart him and make it understandable why he avoids it." Throughout his schooling, he rarely read for pleasure. But at age 26, while on vacation, he picked up *The Road* by Cormack McCarthy, recommended to him by his mother. He finished it in a day and immediately went on to read two other books by the same author. His mother believed that it was ". . . all those years that his dad and I read wonderful books aloud to him that finally paid off."

Carlos was diagnosed with dyslexia and an expressive language impairment at a young age, but even boys without disabilities struggle with reading in the early grades. Because the current push-down academic curriculum is not in sync with the developmental capacities of many young boys, they are at greater risk than girls of being perceived and seeing themselves as academic failures, particularly in regard to reading and writing. To quote one articulate kindergarten boy, "I don't like school. The work is too hard!"

All boys are entitled to a classroom climate that enables them to establish and maintain self-esteem and confidence in themselves as "learners." In the absence of a supportive climate, boys who struggle with literacy acquisition are very likely to turn away from books, actively choosing to be nonreaders rather than expose themselves to ridicule, a phenomenon well articulated by Herbert Kohl in his classic essay "I Won't Learn From You"

(1994). In this essay, Kohl talks about Barry, a child who had been placed in Kohl's combined kindergarten/first-grade class after being held back from moving on to second grade. Barry had a tantrum the first time Kohl asked him to read and, as Kohl discovered, had been able to avoid reading throughout the previous school year by consistently displaying such behavior. Kohl intuited that Barry was capable of learning to read and found a way to begin to engage him without shaming him for not yet reading. The essay speaks to what Kohl refers to as the role of assent in learning. He believed that Barry, an African American boy, as well as other boys of color described in his essay, resisted passive submission to authority and would only become engaged if they could take ownership of their own learning. This resistance, according to Kohl, was in part a response to the way these boys were perceived by their White teachers (1994, pp. 8–10).

THE IMPACT OF THE PUSH-DOWN ACADEMIC CURRICULUM

Twenty years ago, Shepard and Smith (1989) conducted a comprehensive analysis of research on retention and made a compelling argument that retention was an ineffective way to improve school performance. They pointed to the negative long-term outcomes of retention, including higher juvenile delinquency and school dropout rates, among children who were recommended for retention and retained when compared to students who were recommended for retention but were not retained. Yet these findings have gone largely ignored by educational policymakers. It is now commonplace to test children beginning in the middle elementary grades, and testing has been steadily moving to the lower elementary grades and even kindergarten. Test scores are a primary data source for holding school districts accountable, which often translates into decisions about promotion and retention. Because boys as a group, and particularly boys of color, tend to score lower than girls in both reading and writing, they are at greater risk of being retained. Even in those early childhood settings that do not use achievement tests per se, boys are more likely than girls to be assessed by their teachers as performing below grade level in literacy and, on this basis, more likely to be recommended for retention.

Unfortunately, the increased focus on high-stakes testing has resulted in a nationwide trend toward greater emphasis on teacher-directed, academic instruction in literacy at the early childhood level with the hope that this will result in improved test performance (Meisels, 2007). In half-day preschools included in a research study, close to 20% of the time was spent on literacy and language arts activities; in kindergarten it increased to 28%, and by first grade it was 60% during the first 3 hours of the day; by third grade, it was 48% of a full 6-hour day (Hamre & Pianta, 2007). As discussed in Chapter 5, with so much time devoted to academic activities, there is little time left for open-ended play with accompanying opportunities for physical movement, socialization, and spontaneous language expression, all of which are essential in promoting cognitive and language development.

The absence of sufficient time for gross-motor activity and outdoor play puts boys at a particular disadvantage. Girls outpace boys in regard to early language development and reading achievement, while boys are more active physically (Berk, 2003; Wright, 2006). The hardships awaiting active kindergarten boys continue through the elementary grades. In a study that examined the amount of time allotted for recess and the classroom behavior of 11,000 third graders, Barros, Silver, and Stein (2009) reported that one-third of the children in the study received less than 15 minutes of recess per day, and those children who received more than 15 minutes were seen as better behaved by their teachers. Specifically in regard to literacy, there is a link between behavioral problems and reading problems, although the first is not necessarily the cause of the second (Snow, 2007).

Although some young children may be ready to learn specific literacy skills through direct instruction, such instruction is not synonymous with literacy development. In a book originally published in 1988, a bygone era when play had not yet begun to disappear from kindergarten classrooms, Judith Schickedanz (1999) pointed out that literacy development begins in infancy and is inextricably connected to language development, which in turn is fostered through play. More recently, Genishi and Dyson (2009) urged early childhood educators to move away from scripted literacy curricula and refocus on children's natural and spontaneous capacities to engage in sociodramatic play and storytelling as the foundation for promoting literacy.

In cognitive developmental terms, Piaget (1954) characterized the capacity to think symbolically as the hallmark of the transition from the first stage of cognitive development, sensorimotor operations, to the second stage, known as preoperations. One way in which this capacity to think symbolically is evidenced is in children's sociodramatic play where they take on different roles, be it mother, father, dog, Spider-Man, or baby, and when they dramatize events that are not actually occurring at the moment. The child's use of language is also evidence of symbolic thought.

When children begin to use words to represent people, objects, and events that are not present at the moment, it shows that they are drawing upon mental images. Upon entry to preschool and kindergarten, children are still linguistic novices and need opportunities to play in order to hone their symbolic capacities, including expressive and receptive language.

In a Piagetian framework, the capacity to read and write can be understood as a secondary or even a tertiary symbol system—the primary system being spoken language and the second, representational art. It follows that, in the early school years, when children's language capacities are still quite rudimentary, emphasis on the direct instruction of literacy (reading and writing) must not undermine or take the place of activities that promote language development. This is of particular concern when thinking about boys, whose language development lags behind that of girls, a challenge that is compounded for boys for whom English is a second language.

PROMOTING AND SUSTAINING BOYS' INTEREST IN LITERACY

There is nothing formulaic about teaching literacy. If there were only one effective way to learn to read and write, children would have remained illiterate for centuries until that one way was discovered (Smith, 1988; Halle, Calkins, Berry, & Johnson, 2003). In early childhood classrooms, it is typical to see a host of strategies intended to help children learn to read and write. While all of these may work with some children, it is unlikely that any one strategy will be effective with all children.

There is a vast body of professional literature on teaching literacy. Typically, pre-service teachers take at least one course in which they study such literature, and for in-service teachers, there is a notable focus on literacy in staff development programs. Because pre-service and in-service teachers have multiple opportunities to learn about these practices and because approaches to teaching literacy continue to evolve, the strategies suggested in this chapter do not delve deeply into literacy instruction per se. Instead, the focus is on promoting and sustaining young boys' interest in books even when they are not yet ready to read. The emphasis is on the need for teachers to become better informed about the vast body of children's literature that exists and to combine this with their efforts to come to know the particular interests of the boys in their classes. By affirming boys' interests through careful selection of children's literature, teachers can enhance the social-emotional classroom climate of the class-room, keeping all boys invested in books, even those who are not yet ready to learn to read.

In early childhood classrooms, skills-based instruction that emerges directly from the child's self-chosen activities and is an adjunct to those activities will facilitate language development rather than arrest it. For example, when a boy working in the block area announces that he has built a garage, the teacher can engage in a conversation with the boy about the garage. She could ask how many cars it will hold, how they will enter and leave, and then see if the boy would like to make a sign that says "garage." If he already knows how to write letters, the teacher can dictate these to the boy. If not, she can write the word and say each letter as she writes. In the professional literature on literacy instruction, this approach is known as emergent literacy and is still promoted in classrooms that are able to engage in child-centered, play-based instruction.

As discussed in Chapter 1, there is evidence that children see reading books as a feminine activity, perhaps because they have few opportunities in school or at home to see men reading (Berk, 2003; Porche, Ross, & Snow, 2004). This makes it particularly important for teachers to find ways to draw boys in as voluntary readers even as they struggle with decoding. The goal is to help them develop and retain a lifelong interest in reading for pleasure.

The classroom library is a primary source of reading material for children. It follows that teachers should pay close attention to stocking and restocking its shelves so that all of the boys in the classroom find books of interest to "read." However, because teachers in early childhood classrooms are predominantly female, the book selections they make for their students may be strongly influenced by their own gender sensibilities and biases. Furthermore, the recent emphasis on literacy instruction in the early grades has resulted in classroom libraries that often emphasize leveled reading books with controlled vocabularies, many of which contain dull stories and misleading illustrations. It is critical to refocus on finding wonderful children's books with beautiful and salient illustrations that will engage boys.

Teachers should make a deliberate effort to expand their repertoire. For example, books about animals, transportation, adventure, sports, and humor may appeal to many boys, but teachers should be mindful that there will be boys who have other interests and that all boys can benefit from books that focus on feelings and friendship.

The aim is to entice boys into the joy of "reading" from the moment they enter the classroom. At a conference on boys and reading, children's book authors and illustrators, most of whom were men, shared their insights about pulling boys into children's literature (Zehr, 2009). Suggestions included creating a sense of intimacy in the illustrations and communicating unconditional love even when characters "mess up."

OBSERVING TO UNCOVER STUDENTS' ACTUAL INTERESTS

Without yet knowing the reading capacities of the actual boys who will be in the class, it is prudent at the beginning of the school year, even in first and second grade, to include a variety of picture books and other reading material on a wide range of topics that can be enjoyed both by boys who can read and those boys who can't.

However, even the first day of school is not too early for teachers to begin to use observation techniques to learn about the specific interests of the boys in the class as well as their capacities to read and to listen. When boys are free to select books, what do they choose? Are there certain books they stay with for long periods? Do they dwell on particular illustrations? Are there books they go back to time after time? Do they show interest in particular topics? By using running records and developing checklists (see Chapter 7) to document boys' book selections as well as their play themes, teachers can ascertain boys' interests and book choices, which will inform the restocking of the classroom library (Lynch-Brown & Tomlinson, 2005).

There is also evidence that boys and girls read differently. In the literature review for a study on how boys and girls respond to literacy, an undergraduate student at the College of New Jersey points to evidence that girls read for enjoyment and boys "read for information or to learn how to do something" (Pender, 2009). Teachers can be on the lookout to see if this finding bears out for the boys in their class and then continue to identify books that encompass such male interests. At the conference mentioned earlier, authors and illustrators offered insights about what they do to deliberately appeal to boys. According to Zehr (2009), who shared those insights in an article for *Education Week*, "Boys like to read books about trucks, boys who get in trouble, sports, animals, and war. More than girls they lean to nonfiction. And don't forget the humor or actions stories" (para. 1).

Teachers can also listen to boys' conversations and record running records or jot down quick anecdotes that reveal what the boys find interesting. Observing during open-ended play activities in the classroom and on the playground can reveal the imaginary roles they like to assume. Do they repeatedly pretend to be Spider-Man or a well-known athlete? Do they engage in pretend gun play or like to assume the role of "bad guy"? This kind of play may primarily reflect the need to feel powerful at an age when so many aspects of boys' lives are controlled by adults. But they may also be practicing what they perceive to be the male role of "instrumental competence" in stereotyped ways, borrowing from the preponderance of images of male machismo that mass media so readily supply. Furthermore, young boys are likely to be aware of current events, knowing that there are wars going on in various places in the world. When war themes emerge as boys engage in sociodramatic play, it is wise to introduce well-written books that address the topic in age-appropriate ways. For example, *My Big Brother* by Miriam Cohen deals in a very sensitive and realistic way with how a young boy copes when his older brother joins the armed services.

Another important observational strategy is embedded in an assignment in a graduate course on children's literature at the early childhood level (Feldman, 2008). Students were asked to choose a book to read to a young child they knew well and then write up a description of the child's responses. They were also asked to reflect on the book they selected and consider whether they might now choose something different. This assignment points to how adults can make their best guesses about books that will be of interest to a particular child but need to take the next step and notice how the child actually responds to the book.

Once the teacher has a sense of the specific interests of the boys in her class, she can again turn to reference books on children's literature or consult with the school librarian for suggestions about books to add to the classroom library.

HELPING BOYS MAKE BOOK SELECTIONS

Including books in the classroom library that are of interest can contribute to boys' self-esteem. This sense can be deepened when teachers are explicit about their own interest in what is of interest to their male students.

When *William's Doll* by Charlotte Zolotow was first published in the 1970s, it was a rarity to have a story about a boy who wanted a doll to play with. When the story was read to a class of 4-year-olds for the first time, the teacher got no reaction from the children. However, after several readings of the book, both girls and boys began to discuss the nurturing things their fathers did for them—"my daddy gave me a bath," "my daddy made me a hamburger." Whereas before children freely spoke about the things their mommies did, *William's Doll* freed them up to talk about the nurturing things their fathers did for them.

By offering suggestions to the whole class early in the school year about how to find books that interest them, the teacher will encourage boys to notice books more acutely and to become more self-aware (Leipzig, personal communication, May 2009). Books in the classroom library can be introduced, the cover and some illustrations shown, with a brief description of topic, characters, and so on. The teacher can also make direct reference to the name of the author or illustrator and point out other books that they have written or illustrated that have been in or will be added to the classroom library. Ideally, the library shelves will allow the front cover of the book to be displayed so that children who cannot yet read can easily find the books that the teacher has introduced and other books with cover illustrations that appeal to them.

Boys' capacities to select books of interest can be further advanced by engaging them in conversations about the books they choose. For example, the teacher can say, "I noticed that you were reading *Mike Mulligan and His Steam Shovel* by Virginia Lee Burton. Did you like it? What did you like about it? I know some other books by that same author. Would you like me to find that book and add it to our library?" Virginia Lee Burton wrote this and other books about large machines specifically for her sons, but the machines have female names, which may contribute to their appeal to girls as well as boys. (See Appendix B for annotations on this and other books by Burton.) After securing the book, the teacher can follow up by telling the boy, "I found that book I talked to you about it. I am interested in what you think of it." She can read it aloud to him individually and/or to the whole class before putting it on the library shelf for this boy and other children to read on their own.

Even when engaged in direct instruction of literacy skills, there are ways to tap boys' need for physical activity. For example, a phonics instruction approach, created by an experienced teacher in Scotland, was designed specifically to address the needs of active boys. Magnetic letters were provided and boys were encouraged to use them to create words. The boys were not introduced to "book reading" until they were able to use 16 different letters to create at least 40 new words. This approach was introduced to kindergarten-age boys who were followed through the equivalent of fifth grade. In comparison to boys who received a blend of phonics (but no magnetic letters) and whole-language instruction, the boys who used magnetic letters were more advanced readers by the end of the second year of the study, and this difference persisted through the primary grades. Furthermore, by the equivalent of fourth grade, the boys who had been introduced to magnetic letters in kindergarten were more advanced in reading than girls their age (Watson study cited in Tyre, 2008).

STRATEGIES

The strategies listed below are intended to foster boys' interest in books and in the process of reading and writing, even before they are ready to learn the skills of encoding and decoding written language. These strategies will continue to be salient for boys, even after they have begun to read and write.

Build a classroom library that includes books that are typically of interest to boys. Reference books on children's literature are a good starting place for identifying books representing a broad array of topics that will interest boys. (See Appendix A for Selected Reference Books on Children's Literature.) Include books from categories such as adventure and mystery, animals, beginning readers, fantasy, folk and fairy tales, humor, and sports.

Include other boy-friendly reading materials in the library. For all boys, and particularly for boys who are already readers, the library should extend beyond children's literature to include magazines and graphic novels covering topics such as superheroes, sports, and mythological characters.

Include books that address feelings of friendship and empathy among boys. Teachers need to be on the lookout for books that affirm feelings that boys may otherwise choose to deny because of gender stereotypes.

Include books about boys and families from diverse racial/ethnic/cultural backgrounds. The classroom library should also include books that explicitly represent the racial/ethnic/cultural backgrounds of boys in the class. This will affirm their developing sense of identity and promote appreciation of diversity among all the students in the class.

Include books about boys and men with nonstereotypic interests. Because there are many boys whose interests are not in keeping with stereotypic male interests, it is essential to include books about boys with nonstereotypic interests.

Incorporate multimedia approaches—for example, listening centers, computer software, Internet activities. Use multimedia, multisensory approaches to actively engage boys in literacy activities, such as listening to a recorded story with the book in hand, writing and drawing on the computer, using software that encourages written letter/word and spoken letter/word connections.

Use an Internet search engine to find Web sites created specifically to engage boys in reading. Conducting an Internet search using descriptors such as "guys read," "books for boys," and "nonsexist books" can uncover interesting Web sites and professional articles on these topics.

Build in time for independent "reading." Build a time into the daily schedule when children can choose books to explore on their own. (In the 1990s, the Drop Everything And Read (DEAR) program promoted this strategy.)

Include read-alouds in the daily schedule. Time should be allotted daily for the teacher to read aloud to the class. Listening to wonderful books is critical in motivating children to learn to read and is a pleasure that does not disappear even after children become independent readers. This is a time for teachers to be particularly mindful of choosing books that will appeal to boys.

Invite male readers into the classroom. Fathers, grandfathers, and other male family members as well as male teachers, teacher aides, administrators, and custodians can be invited to share a favorite book or to read a book that the teacher suggests. If the family member is not comfortable reading aloud, he can be asked to "talk the story" to the children, using the illustrations as cues to the storyline.

Enlist upper-grade boys as book buddies. Pair older boys who enjoy reading with younger boys who seem disinterested in books. This can reassure young boys that reading is something that is enjoyable and an appropriate activity for boys. It is also worthwhile to pair older boys and younger boys who share the same interests, such as a particular sport, animals, or adventure.

Use techniques of observing and recording to uncover boys' interests. Techniques for observing and recording children's behavior, such as running records, anecdotes, and checklists can be used to document boys' interests (see Chapter 7). Book selections for the classroom library and decisions about methods for effectively engaging boys in literacy activities can be informed by observational data.

CONCLUSION

Although there may be good reasons to teach literacy skills in the early grades, the extent to which these activities have come to dominate the schedule in early childhood classrooms puts boys at a disadvantage, particularly if their developmental capacities, while in keeping with norms for their gender, are not in keeping with the heavy emphasis on teaching academic skills. The research cited in this chapter points to the flaws in presuming that increasing the amount of time for literacy in the early grades will automatically produce better readers later on. What is called for is a different balance between teacher-directed instructional time and child-initiated activities. In addition, teachers must be ever mindful about ways to support boys even if they are not ready to read. The provision of an expansive classroom library of wonderful books on a range of topics as well as other kinds of reading material of interest to boys will go a long way toward motivating them to learn to decode in the short run and to see themselves as independent readers for a lifetime.

FOR FURTHER REFLECTION

- What are the specific interests of the boys in the class? Does the classroom library reflect these interests?
- How can the daily schedule be altered to build in time for children to explore books independently and for the teacher to read aloud to the class?
- When is there time for conversations with individual boys about their interests and book preferences?
- Who are the males who can be invited to come to the classroom to read to the class or with individual boys?

KEY READINGS

Genishi, C., & Dyson, A. H. (2009). *Children, language and literacy: Diverse learners in diverse times.* New York: Teachers College Press.

   The authors urge early childhood educators to turn away from direct instruction and refocus on expressive activities such as sociodramatic play, storytelling, and creative arts as a way to promote language and literacy. They point out that this is particularly critical because of the diversity of linguistic and cultural backgrounds of America's schoolchildren.

Lynch-Brown, C., & Tomlinson, C. M. (2005). *Essentials of children's literature.* Boston: Pearson.

   The first section of this book will help teachers think about the meaning and value of literature to children. The rest of the book is devoted to different genres of literature, with a list of recommended books. A chapter devoted to picture books is particularly relevant at the early childhood level.

Zher, M. (2009, July 2). Authors share tips on how to hook boys on books. *Education Week.* Retrieved July 11, 2009, from http://www.edweek.org/ew/contributors/mary.zehr.html.

   This article offers wonderful insights from noted children's book authors and illustrators about strategies that they use to engage boys in reading their books.

CHAPTER 5

Active Learning Through Play

Essential Elements for Engaging Boys in Learning

It was table time at a preschool program within a public school. The children were working on mandated readiness activities, coloring in worksheets to teach numeracy. The activity was supposed to last 20 minutes, but after 5 minutes Jake and Tyrone, who had recently turned 5 and were good friends, were fidgeting. They were dropping markers on the floor, squirming around in their seats, and generally acting antsy. Tyrone actually fell on the floor at one point. Their teacher tried to keep them focused and frequently asked them to "sit up straight," and reminded them more than once, "This is work time, focus." When the children handed in their "work," the teacher noticed that neither boy had finished the math page, which added to her perception that these two boys were not doing well.

A 30-minute "choice time" followed "work time." Jake and Tyrone chose to work together in the block area. As the teacher floated between centers, she noticed that Jake and Tyrone were totally engaged in building an airport. As they worked, she heard this conversation:

Jake: Ty, I need three more long blocks for the runway.
Ty: There are no more on the shelf.
Jake: Oh, oh.
Ty: I know, we can use more small blocks.
Jake: Yeah, let's use the half-size ones.
Ty: Okay.
[Ty brings four unit blocks over]
Jake: We need two more. That'll be the same as three long ones.
Ty: Yeah, that'll work.

Later in the day, Jake and Tyrone's teacher was thinking about the knowledge of math the boys had displayed during their block play. There was no sign of restlessness or boredom as they problem-solved using math skills such as numeracy, multiplication, and geometry in building their block runway. The scenario she had observed made her realize how far her classroom, with its largely mandated academic curriculum, had strayed from her training and her beliefs about early childhood education. She reflected on principles she had learned in child development courses leading up to her master's degree, remembering how one of her favorite professors had begun a class on child development: "Play is children's work is not a cliché; it is the principle on which early childhood education is founded."

Early childhood educators were supported in their commitment to a play-centered, active-learning curriculum by eminent philosophers and psychologists such as John Dewey, Jean Piaget, and Jerome Bruner, who understood that children need first-hand experience with objects in their environment before they can understand symbols and abstractions for those objects (Dewey, 1938; Piaget, 1954; Bruner, 1969). The writings of these thinkers helped early childhood educators understand that children typically move through developmental stages and that educational practice needs to be appropriate to those stages. The field of early childhood education has been built on the theoretical framework provided by Dewey, Piaget, Bruner, and others who have translated theory into a knowledge base incorporating learning through concrete experience (active learning).

PLAY IS LEARNING

Children are active learners by nature. They learn through experience—they understand the number two by having two crackers, one for each hand. Learning to say "10" means nothing to a child until he or she repeatedly and over time counts 10 fingers, 10 toes, 10 crackers, 10 blocks, or 10 cars. Through concrete experience with counting objects in their world, children learn the meaning of numbers. Children learn colors by relating the name of a color with the shirt they are wearing that day. They know the "l" sound if their name or their mother or father or sister or brother's name begins with the letter "l," and they hear it in their daily lives. They understand the geometric proportion of one building block to another by using blocks to build with on a daily basis. They learn the give and take of social interaction through dramatic play scenarios that reflect real life in terms of family and community. Young children are constantly constructing knowledge based on experiences they have in school, at home, or on a walk to the park or grocery store.

Given that boys typically enter early childhood classrooms less developmentally mature than girls in terms of literacy and social-emotional skills, providing ample opportunity for them to engage in all forms of play is critical. Play allows boys to move about physically in the classroom and outdoors, to express themselves through a variety of dramatic play scenarios, and to learn how to negotiate social-emotional situations through interactions with peers and adults. As Miller and Almon (2009) report,

> Young children work hard at play. They invent scenes and stories, solve problems, and negotiate their way through social roadblocks. They know what they want to do and work diligently to do it. Because their motivation comes from within, they learn the powerful lesson of pursuing their own ideas to a successful conclusion. (p. 7)

If preschool and kindergarten provide opportunities for a wide range of free and guided play experiences that are then reinforced through developmentally appropriate curriculum, children will be ready to read and write and negotiate social situations more successfully when they move up to the primary grades. As a matter of fact, play experiences enrich vocabulary and other emerging literacy skills, as well as social-emotional learning that lead to greater success in the early primary grades.

Scheduling ample play periods into the daily schedule allows children's play to develop more sophistication, evolving from play with objects to a more mature form of pretend play. Engaging in this form of dramatic play, children take on roles and behaviors, using their imaginations to create situations and interactions that further their understanding of the world around them and, at the same time, build their vocabularies and other language skills (Bedrova & Leong, 2003).

One only needs to carefully observe the complexity of children's dramatic play to know that cognitive curriculum and play are not mutually exclusive aspects of early childhood education. It is the teacher's role to develop, guide, and facilitate children's play so that it advances their cognitive and social-emotional skill development. As Hyson (2003) states, "Without a nurturing, playful responsive environment, an academic focus may diminish children's engagement and motivation. But a 'child-centered' environment that lacks intellectual challenges also falls short of what curious young learners deserve" (p. 23). Elkind (2006) urges parents and teachers to step back and let children learn at their own pace by using their imaginations and engaging in play.

BOYS AND
EARLY ACADEMICS

The concept of free and guided play to advance cognitive development is especially critical for boys who need a learning environment that challenges them in developmentally appropriate ways rather than making them fit into a more formal structure that works against their developmental needs. The standards movement and its corollary, high-stakes testing, have had an impact on early childhood education in ways that can have a detrimental effect on boys. Principles of developmentally appropriate practice (Copple & Bredekamp, 2009), which give equal weight to social-emotional, physical, and cognitive development, have yielded to seat work, worksheets, and other highly structured lessons, often beginning in preschool. Pushing down the kind of curriculum that was once the province of first and second grade results in anxiety and a sense of failure for many children, and most particularly boys. For too many boys, this sense of not measuring up can dampen their enthusiasm for learning and stifle the boundless energy that they bring into their preschool or kindergarten class. In an ideal learning environment, periods of play would be built into the daily schedule in grades 1–3 as well as in pre-K and kindergarten.

Instead of viewing boys' energy as an asset, many teachers see it as a negative trait that disrupts the culture of the classroom. Too often, teachers spend a great deal of time trying to tamp down this energy rather than helping boys find successful ways to use it as a learning tool. When deprived of physical activity such as recess and the opportunity for active play in the classroom, boys show signs of stress, anger, aggression, and depression. Acting out these negative feelings often results in behaviors that can lead to expulsion, suspension, or a recommendation for medicating the child (Miller & Almon, 2009). Given what is known about boys' need for physical activity, the inappropriateness of the academic kindergarten is very clear.

ADDRESSING THE "CRISIS" IN EARLY CHILDHOOD EDUCATION

Miller and Almon (2009) maintain that the situation for young children deprived of a play–centered learning environment in early childhood has reached crisis proportions. Their report states that, on a typical day, children in all-day kindergartens spend 2 to 3 hours per day in literacy, math, and test-prep activities and as little as 30 minutes per day in choice-time activities. It minces no words:

> Kindergartners are now under great pressure to meet inappropriate expectations, including academic standards that until recently were reserved for first grade. At the same time, they are being denied the benefits of play—a major stress reliever. This double burden, many experts believe, is contributing to a rise in anger and aggression in young children, reflected in increasing reports of severe behavior problems. (p. 11)

Research supports the position that a play-centered curriculum has long-term benefits for children. The High/Scope Preschool Curriculum longitudinal study conducted in the 1970s was the first to show that over time children who had a play-centered preschool experience did better in terms of personal relations, educational levels attained, and job and career success (High/Scope Research Foundation, as cited in Miller & Almon, 2009).

Another study, conducted in Germany, compared 50 play-based classrooms with 50 early learning centers. The results showed that the children in play-based centers excelled academically, and were better adjusted in terms of social-emotional development. The German children in play-based settings also scored higher in creativity, verbal ability, and attention to work (German study, as cited in Miller & Almon, 2009).

BACK TO BASICS

After a long period in which the "push-down" curriculum has held sway, there is a growing awareness that the academic early childhood classroom does not serve the needs of young children, especially young boys. The Alliance for Childhood, the National Black Child Development Institute, and the National Association for the Education of Young Children have taken a leadership role in reasserting the importance of child development, with a focus on active learning through play.

A teacher described a brief piece of special curriculum that really helped a kindergarten boy who was known to have emotional difficulties and often seemed disengaged from classroom activities. One day, he came into school with a measuring tape. He kept fiddling with the tape until the teacher suggested that they use it to measure things in the classroom. It only took a few minutes to measure objects of his choice and write down the numbers. Later that day, the boy and his teacher created a book about the experience. They called it *Yonni's Measuring Story*. He was very proud of his book, especially when the teacher read it to the whole class. A few minutes of personal attention went a long way to create a sense of belonging for Yonni.

For early childhood educators, the comprehensive guidelines for the education of children ages birth through 8 years can be found in *Developmentally Appropriate Practice* issued by the National Association for the Education of Young Children (Copple & Bredekamp, 2009). The guidelines address the concept of educating the whole child: recognizing developmental stages and individual differences in maturation, the influence of the social and cultural context of the child on learning, the importance of active learning through play, the appreciation of different learning styles,

A preschool teacher attending a workshop on teasing and bullying shared her strategy for giving boys a way to expend energy and satisfy their need for rough-and-tumble play. She called it "rug wrestling." The teacher put a small rug and a timer in one area of the classroom. Two children at a time were able to kneel on the rug and engage in physical play (wrestling) for 2 to 3 minutes. The rules were that you had to line up near the rug if you wanted a turn, and willingly move off the rug when your time was up. She reported that this simple outlet was fun for the children, especially boys, and dramatically reduced incidents of verbal conflicts and physical fighting.

and the essential need to provide each child with a safe and nurturing environment. The latest edition segments the guidelines into infant/toddler, preschool, kindergarten, and primary grades, but at every stage the importance of play and social-emotional development is emphasized.

STRATEGIES

The challenge for pre-K–3 teachers is to find ways to design a learning environment that is more developmentally appropriate and attuned to the needs of boys. Strategies to help them be more successful during mandated activities, and to facilitate active learning through play within the school day follow:

Give a short (1- to 2-minute) exercise break before and after a mandated activity. Jumping jacks can expend a lot of energy, and if the activity is a math worksheet, children can exercise and reinforce what is on the sheet at the same time. For example, "Do 10 jumping jacks, counting aloud as you do them; jump three times for three cats and six times for six cats."

Create an "exercise area" in the classroom where boys and girls can go when they feel the need for physical activity. The area can have some pictures of yoga activities and a mat for sit-ups. Display a chart of the rules for the area and go over them during a class meeting so children understand how the space is to be used. Put an egg timer in the space so children know that they need to return to work when the timer runs out. If possible, extend the work period by the same amount of time for a child who has used the exercise area.

Create a "stand-up" place to do seatwork. Set worksheets up on a shelf that will allow boys (and girls) to focus better if they can stand instead of sit. A teacher in a Midwest middle school found this to be a very successful strategy for middle school boys who had difficulty sitting still for work periods.

Teach children who get antsy to stand for a few seconds and take some deep breaths. Again, counting can be incorporated into the activity—for example, "Count to five (hold up one finger for each number); now take five deep breaths (again holding up a finger for each breath), now sit down."

Create play reports as a way to keep play in the curriculum and also meet the mandates. After choice time, have children report back verbally and then write or dictate a story about what they did and illustrate it. Stress speaking in whole sentences during report back time, and highlight new vocabulary learned. Words that are new for everyone can be put up on a word wall. Review the play reports with boys who have trouble focusing. Use the reports to affirm for them how much they are learning, and relate the skills to work time literacy or math lessons. Keep these reports as part of children's work portfolios and share them with parents at conference time.

Create a fact sheet for parents that will help them understand the importance of play as a learning tool for young children, especially boys. Cite some research, which makes the case irrefutable (see examples in this chapter), and give references if parents want to read more on their own.

Devote a small segment of recess (about 10 minutes) to structured learning games for boys. For example, a spelling race (how many words that end in "at" can you spell, followed by a chance to run around the playground as many times), or a math challenge version of Simon Says (Simon says, "Take three plus two steps" or "two times two steps"). If the idea catches on, boys can be encouraged to make up outdoor learning games of their own and write or draw instructions that others can follow.

Look for an area of interest, such as sports or science fiction, and build curriculum around it. If the interest is science fiction, for example, convert the dramatic play area into a spaceship or space station. Cardboard cartons, aluminum foil, and imagination on the part of children and teachers can create a whole unit on space exploration. Have children write or dictate and illustrate space stories, or create a space mural for the classroom during art time (or with the art specialist). If the original idea came from a boy, encourage him to take a leadership role in the activities. In grades 1–3, select books about space exploration and biographies of astronauts from the library, have children conduct simple Internet research, create a word wall of space vocabulary, and write poetry and songs about space travel.

Engage boys in creating and directing a play. This can be a confidence-builder and a successful literacy activity for a boy who is not yet ready to read. The idea for the play can come from something that is going on in the classroom, such as a playground incident, or an upcoming trip. It is important to set ground rules for plays—no children's names can be used; the characters have to be animals; no swear words; and so on.

Use outdoor time for quick science experiments. For example, set up some ramps of different heights (using blocks or large pieces of cardboard propped against a bench) and toy cars of different sizes. Ask boys to predict how far they think certain cars will travel on each ramp, and then test their prediction. Back in the classroom, ask boys to explain the experiment and the results. In grades 1–3, the experiment can be charted on a bar graph and hypotheses can be made based on making the ramps higher or lower, and then testing them.

CONCLUSION

In recent years, early childhood education has veered from a play-centered to an academic-centered pre-K–3 learning environment. However, the literature makes it clear that play is an essential learning tool for all children, and a critical element in keeping boys engaged in learning. The move toward early academics has been particularly hard on boys, asking them to perform tasks that they are not developmentally ready for, and creating a sense of failure before they even reach first grade. The *Crisis in the Kindergarten* report provides chapter and verse on the harm that is being done. The writers of the report, Edward Miller and Joan Almon, are joined in advocating for a play-centered approach by eminent psychologists such as David Elkind, researchers and teacher educators such as Elena Bodrova and Deborah Leong, and leaders of major early childhood organizations such as the National Association for the Education of Children and the National Black Child Development Institute.

It is important to understand that a playful learning environment does not mean that children are not acquiring a range of skills that are necessary for success in school. On the contrary, they are constructing cognitive and social-emotional skills in myriad ways through their interactions with materials, peers, teachers, and other adults in the school community.

Based on the research, one could argue that boys' engagement in learning and success in school would be greater if the curriculum in grades 1–3 continued to meet their needs for physical activity, social-emotional skill development, and "playful" learning. Meeting these critical needs is one underutilized long-term strategy for closing the achievement gap and dropout rate that limits the future potential of far too many boys.

FOR FURTHER REFLECTION

- How and where in the school might there be support for keeping play in the K–3 classroom? Is there a Community of Practice? Is it possible to start one?
- What are some practical ways to help parents understand the importance of play as a tool for learning?
- What are some strategies for channeling boys' energy as a tool for learning?

KEY READINGS

Bodrova, E., & Leong, D. J. (2003). The importance of being playful. *Educational Leadership, 60*(7), 50–53.

> *This article speaks about the effects of play on early learning and development and defines the characteristics and positive effects of mature play. It also addresses the important role of teachers in guiding play and helping children advance their play over time.*

Elkind, D. (2006). *The power of play: How spontaneous, imaginative activities lead to happier healthier children.* Cambridge, MA: De Capo Press.

> *A key message is the vast amount of learning that comes from unstructured play and discovery and the developmental benefits of different types of play. The book argues that video games, TV, and computers take valuable play time away from children.*

Hyson, M. (2003). Putting early academics in their place. *Educational Leadership, 60*(7), 20–23.

> *This article takes a measured view for combining academics with play and a focus on social-emotional skill development. Hyson argues that all three components are important and can be successfully accomplished in early childhood programs.*

Miller, E., & Almon, J. (2009). *The crisis in kindergarten: Why children need to play in school.* College Park, MD: Alliance for Childhood.

> *This report is a rallying cry for returning kindergarten to its roots as a year for developing social-emotional skills in a playful learning environment. The National Advisory Board of the Alliance for Childhood includes leading national educators in the field and representatives from major universities, all of whom are advocates for principles of child development.*

CHAPTER 6

School, Family, and Community Partnerships

Key to Boys' Success in School

It is parent conference time for the third grade in the Franklin Avenue School. There is a tense atmosphere in the school because teachers are preparing children for the third-grade reading test that is coming up in the spring. At one teacher/mother conference, the following takes place.

T: Good afternoon, Ms. Gordon. I'm glad you could come in today. First of all, I want you to know that I think Jeffrey is a very nice child. The other children like him and he is a good sport. But frankly, I'm worried about his skills. Right now, he's not reading at grade level, and he often doesn't pay attention during literacy activities. I'd like to see him do well on the upcoming test and of course I want the whole class to do well.

Ms. G: I try to teach him good manners. What can I do about his reading? I don't have much time to work with him at home. I just get home from work in time to make dinner, get the kids bathed, and put them to bed.

T: I know how hard it must be, but it's really important for you to work with him at home. I'm going to give you some drills that we use in class, and you will have to find time to do them with him every night. I think that will help him score higher and improve the class ranking as a whole. Thanks for coming in.

For parents of boys, being asked to come to school to talk to the teacher too often means they are going to hear something negative, which sets up a situation that is not beneficial for the teachers, the parents, and especially

54

not for the boys. Not only does it create negative feelings for the child, but it also may lead to punishment at home.

BOYS NEED POSITIVE SCHOOL/FAMILY CONNECTIONS

Parents, family members, and other caregivers need to be engaged in the challenge of making school a more successful experience for boys. Too often, they are only expected to become involved when problems arise. The hastily called conference "to discuss Joe's disruptive behavior" or "Jamal's low reading score" is all too familiar.

Imagine a different teacher/parent conference for the same child:

T: Hello, Ms. Gordon. Thanks for coming in tonight. I can imagine how difficult it is for you to get away around dinner time after a full day at your job. Who's with the children?

Ms. G: My sister came over to stay with the kids. She helps me a lot. How's Jeffrey doing?

T: He is well behaved and he is a good sport, which makes him very well liked by the other children. One thing we do need to do is improve his reading skills. Does he do any reading at home?

Ms. G: Not really. We don't have too many books around, and I don't have much time for stories. To tell the truth, I turn on the TV a lot.

T: Well, if we're going to get Jeffrey up to speed for his own sake and for the upcoming reading test, we'll both have to work with him. Tell me about his interests. What does he like?

Ms. G: Well, he always watches adventure stuff on TV, and when my brother comes over, they watch basketball games.

T: Okay. That gives me an idea. Jeffrey and I are going to take a trip to the school library on my prep period. I'll ask the librarian to have a selection of adventure and sports stories picked out, and he can choose one book to take home. Your job is to sit with him while he reads at least three pages every day, including weekends. Help him with words he doesn't know. Point out the beginning letter, look at the pictures, and help him sound out the word. When a child is learning to read, everything is a clue. Each time he finishes a book, he and I will meet to talk about it, and he'll get to choose another one. He can keep a log of books he has read at home. Let's try that for 2 months, and then we can either meet or talk on the telephone about his progress.

Ms. G: Since he's older, I can let him stay up a little longer, so we can read just before bedtime. I'll be glad to do that if it will help him read.

T: I'm sure it will. The time alone with you will be important. Our goal is to get this boy to enjoy reading. Thanks again for coming in.

These two scenarios reveal much about the variations in teacher attitudes toward parents and also about children, especially boys. The teacher in the first conference conveys tension about her class measuring up during the test. Perhaps she is inexperienced or just insecure. She seems wedded to a drill approach to reading, and perpetuates Jeffrey's reading problem by sending home more of what isn't working in school. She also doesn't ask for or expect any input from Jeffrey's mother. She just tells her what she *must* do.

The teacher in the second scenario has a completely different approach. She conveys to Ms. G. knowledge and understanding of a single, working mother's life. At the same time, she knows that she must engage this woman in the campaign to improve her son's reading skills. She involves Jeffrey's mother in identifying her son's interests and bases her strategy to engage him in reading on this information. In addition, this teacher is willing to give up a bit of her prep time to pay special attention to this child, who seems to get little of it at home. And, finally, she also finds a way for Jeffrey's mother to carve out a special piece of time for him. There is a sense of partnership and positive gain all around from her approach.

Unfortunately, conferences with a teacher and parent working together to find out a child's interests as a way to improve his reading are all too rare. Yet, developing a sense of partnership between home and school is essential if children are to build trusting relationships that free them to learn. A boy who doesn't feel that sense of community, who feels anxious when his parent is asked to come to school, or has picked up on an attitude that says "your family is not okay," is a boy who cannot be expected to feel safe, welcome, or trusting of the school environment. Unfortunately, this is the case for many boys at every level of education. If this disassociation begins in early childhood, it becomes predictable that it will continue and increase, resulting in low achievement and early dropout.

A classroom teacher plays a key role in fostering positive parent/family/community relationships that enable children, and especially boys, to feel a positive connection to the world inside and outside of the school. The communication set up between home and school benefits children in myriad ways: Research shows that they do better academically (Henderson & Mapp, 2002), it supports their social-emotional development and sense of trust in adults, it creates a sense of belonging to the larger world (Bowman & Moore, 2006), and it affirms that the child's home is important and respected (Day, 2006).

FORMING A HOME/SCHOOL PARTNERSHIP

Parent/family involvement is an essential aspect of a child's success in school (Henderson & Mapp, 2002; Epstein et al., 2009; Keyser, 2006). Studies at the preschool level have shown that when families work in partnership the gain is two-way: Teachers become more sensitive and understanding of the children in their classrooms and parents become more supportive of children's learning (Taylor & Machida, as cited in Riley, San Juan, Klinkner & Ramminger, 2008). Similar results have been reported for first grade (Reynolds, as cited in Riley et al., 2008) and in another longitudinal study children's educational attainment at age 25 was predictable based on their parents' involvement at age 7 (Flouri & Buchanan, as cited in Riley et al., 2008).

VIEWING PARENTS/FAMILY MEMBERS AS ASSETS

The first step in creating positive family involvement is to view it as an asset to teaching, and create a comfort level for parents and other family members. It is important to keep in mind that for many parents, especially those who are recent immigrants or for whom English is not their first language, coming into school for a conference can be an intimidating experience. Even middle-class families can feel apprehensive based on their own school experiences.

Creating an atmosphere of welcome can become an asset in many ways. Parents and other family members can provide insight into a boy's likes and dislikes, how he responds to challenges, what relationships are most important to him within the family, and what causes him feelings of stress. These insights can help shape learning that fits the needs of each individual child. Also, if they are made to feel welcome, parents and other family members can bring special talents and skills into the classroom.

Tapping into the talent within families can bring amazing resources into the classroom. And children feel valued when someone from their family is part of their learning environment.

Most important for a boy is finding out who the positive males are in his life, and engaging those men in his education. It may be a father living with the family or not, an uncle, a grandfather, an older brother, or a family friend. It also could be someone from the community such as a Big Brother or a coach. Such role models can have an enormous influence, helping to keep a boy focused on school and presenting a future to which he can aspire. A national study on promoting academic success in boys of color conducted at the Frank Porter Graham Institute addressed the need for intervention on several fronts to help boys in their adjustment to school: family practices that fail to optimize boys' social-emotional and academic development; the limited involvement of fathers and father surrogates; gaps in teacher preparation to work with diverse populations; risky environments; and a lack of fit between school organization and boys' competencies and dispositions.

HOW TO MAKE FAMILY INVOLVEMENT HAPPEN

Riley et al. (2008) provide a list of tips for working successfully with parents/family members. Although tip number one—Discuss your expectations during pre-enrollment meeting or intake interview—is most applicable to pre-K or kindergarten classrooms, tips two through four are universal and applicable to teachers working with students of every age. They include: Take time to build the relationship; in addition to scheduled conferences, use every available moment to communicate personal interest in the parent and child; respect and accept parents; don't bring a premature, judgmental eye to the relationship; learn to understand the cultural context for parenting, and then work together to bridge gaps between school and home; emphasize the positive and always be on the lookout for something to say that is appreciative of some aspect of the parent and focuses on a positive trait in her/his child.

These tips are words of wisdom and also make plain common sense. They are the backbone of building community between school and home. They look to the positive rather than the negative, and can be of enormous benefit to boys.

CULTURAL/LINGUAL
RESPECT

It is important to understand how a child's culture affects his or her approach to school and to incorporate that knowledge in planning for individual and group success in school. Reaching beyond the confines of one's own culture to learn about the diversity of cultures within a classroom can open new approaches to teaching and learning. Communicating with parents about what their families value and celebrate can provide insight into how to structure lessons that capture a child's motivation to learn. Bringing culture into the classroom can energize teaching and learning, and develop children's acceptance of and respect for difference.

Respect for language is integral to respect for culture. The United States is unique in its focus on monolingualism. Almost everywhere else in the world people pride themselves on multilingualism. If there is a genuine desire to welcome family and community members into the school environment, providing information in their home language and translation for conferences and meetings needs to be provided.

A Head Start program on the Lower East Side in New York City was experiencing an influx of new families from Colombia, South America. The staff and director were brainstorming ideas to create a sense of belonging for the children and their families, and came up with the following strategies: They commissioned a craftsperson to create large (toddler-size) boy/girl dolls with facial features that reflected a range of people from Colombia, such as light eye color and various light to dark skin tones, and they invited parents into the center to tell familiar folk tales and/or cook foods that were particular to their culture. The children were delighted to see themselves reflected in the dolls, and the parents were willing and excited to share aspects of their culture with the children. Outreach to fathers as well as mothers led to men participating in the classroom visits.

COMMUNITY SUPPORT

Garbarino (1999) has written extensively about the importance for boys to have support from persons outside the family. All boys, but especially those who live in dysfunctional families and/or communities, need role models and mentors who provide moral support and connections to positive core values. In addition to supportive schools, community-based organizations such as Big Brothers, Boys and Girls Clubs, and houses of worship can provide a sense of belonging and being cared for that can keep a boy on a path to success. Experience has shown that "one caring adult," a person who provides unconditional love and support, can turn a child's life around, setting him or her on a path of success. That person can be a parent, an extended family member, a member of the clergy, a youth worker, or an assigned Big Brother.

STRATEGIES

Here are some ideas to consider for creating school/home/community connections.

Invite parents and family members in to talk about their childhood experiences growing up in different parts of the United States or overseas. Display a large world map on a wall in the classroom and ask family members to mark their home locales. Use pushpins and string to connect everyone's place of origin, creating a picture of the global diversity that the class represents. Send home a copy of the map with each child, and/or invite family members to a classroom celebration of the map.

Design a class project that is geared to boys' interests and involves family and community members. One idea might be a sports party, with a display of sports-related books and snacks such as popcorn. Boys might get engaged in picking sport songs and games as party entertainment. An older brother or sister who is involved in sports could be a guest of honor.

Keep the lines of communication between home and school open through a regular newsletter (available in home languages). Having students contribute to the newsletter is an engaging literacy activity. Boys might want to report on the sports party or write about a book they liked. During the course of a school year, the newsletter can feature a short article on someone from each child's family, and the child can be the interviewer. The newsletter can be made available online and in print.

Keep a camera handy as a helpful home/school communication tool. Parents love to see pictures of their children at work, so regularly take individual and group pictures to send home.

Use the outdoors as a venue for family involvement to address boys' need to be physically active. During nice weather, plan an outdoor sports event that will involve parents, family, and community members in activities such as races and ball games.

Ask parents or family members if they have connections in the community that could be a source for positive male role models. If there are no suggestions, contact local community-based organizations such as Big Brothers/Big Sisters, Boys and Girls Clubs, or the Urban League.

Develop a relationship with the director of a school-based or community-based afterschool program. She or he could be a resource for finding positive role models for boys. Sometimes teenage boys who are active in the center, with guidance from the youth director, can befriend the younger boys. This type of relationship is beneficial for both the teenager and the young boy, provided that it is guided by adults.

CONCLUSION

The partnership between school, home, and community is a key element in boys' success in school. The Henderson and Mapp research addresses this from an educational standpoint, and Bowman, Brunson-Day, and Garbarino from a social-emotional perspective. In the preschool and kindergarten years, communication and cooperation between home and school are at their highest. However, as children go through the grades, communication is usually confined to a curriculum meeting at the beginning of the year and one or two brief conferences. The rich pool of human resources that family and community can provide often are underutilized, or not used at all.

For boys, tapping into these resources can be crucial to success. As described above, a successful male role model or mentor can be the person who keeps a boy focused on his future, showing him options that he might not otherwise know exist. A caring adult—family member, teacher, youth worker, or mentor—affirms a boy's self-worth, letting him know he is a valued person who has a contribution to make to his community and society at large.

FOR FURTHER REFLECTION

- What are the best ways within the school culture to affirm and celebrate the diversity of students and families?
- What type of communication would be most effective in reaching a parent or key family member about a boy who is not faring well—for example, in person, email, written note?
- What resources are available to translate home/school communications into languages other than English?
- What resources are there in the community that can provide role models and mentors for boys?

KEY READINGS

Epstein, J., Sanders, M. G., Sheldon, S. B., Simon, B. S., Salinas, K. C., & Rodriguez-Jansorn, N., et al. (2009). *School, family and community partnerships: Your handbook for action* (3rd ed.). New York: Corwin Press.

> *Joyce Epstein, of the Center for the Social Organization of the Schools, is nationally known for her commitment to family involvement in schools. In this handbook for action, she has assembled experts in the field that tell how to create Action Teams for Partnerships to promote positive family involvement.*

Henderson, A. T., & Mapp, K. L. (2002). *A new wave of evidence: The impact of school, family, and community connections on student achievement*. Austin, TX: Southwest Educational Development Laboratory (National Center for Family & Community Connections).

> *This compendium of studies on the impact of family involvement on children's success in school provides ample evidence of the importance of creating and maintaining positive home/school connections at every level of education.*

Keyser, J. (2006). *From parents to partners: Building a family-centered early childhood program*. St. Paul, MN: Redleaf Press (also available through NAEYC).

> *An excellent reference for ideas about how to make family/school partnerships an integral part of every classroom. Every chapter has practical strategies and questions for self-reflection.*

CHAPTER 7

Observing and Recording Children's Behavior

It has long been the practice in the field of early childhood education to pre-pare prospective teachers to observe and record children's behavior. Since the child study movement took hold in the early part of the 20th century, teachers of young children have been encouraged to observe and record as a way of coming to know each child as an individual. Techniques for observing and recording can also be deliberately employed to examine the role of gender in classroom life, revealing its impact on boys' behavior, social interactions, and activity preferences.

HOLDING JUDGMENT AND PERSONAL REACTIONS IN ABEYANCE

The issues raised in Chapter 1 all indicate that it is up to teachers to find ways to stand back and look at boys' behavior while holding their own judgments and personal reactions in abeyance. By looking for patterns in boys' behaviors and activity preferences as well as variations that may occur in different contexts, it is possible to think more clearly about each boy's behavior from his perspective and to begin to recognize behavior that may reflect the boy's evolving sense of gender identity. Awareness that evolving gender identity is one hypothesis that can explain boys' behavior affords teachers the opportunity to consider responses that can better meet boys' needs without automatically translating their behavior into "pathology." Techniques for observing and recording are invaluable in coming to know the boys in the class as unique individuals, enabling teachers to engage in assessment and curriculum planning informed by an awareness of boys' strengths and needs.

In the process of observing the boys in the class, teachers are also primed to examine their own internalized gender sensibilities that may reflect stereotypic expectations of the society at large. Teachers possess perceptions about gender and race, developed during childhood and carried into their adult lives, and they bring these sensibilities to their interactions with children in classroom settings. These attitudes in turn play a role in shaping young children's developing gender identities.

Although teachers bring their internalized sensibilities about gender and other aspects of identity into the classroom, albeit subconsciously, a hallmark of professionalism is the ability to uncover and examine such beliefs by engaging in what Donald Schon (1983) calls "reflective practice." The techniques for observing, recording, and analyzing children's behavior, included in many early childhood teacher education programs, can be used to help look more closely at children's behavior and simultaneously examine personal reactions to the observed behavior (Cohen, Stern, Balaban, & Gropper, 2008).

It is valuable to take a look at professional literature focused on boys or think of other means of raising teachers' consciousness about the subtle ways in which gender and race/ethnicity can play a role in classroom life and have a negative impact on boys. For example, in a graduate course taught by one of the authors of this book, students are required to observe, record, and analyze the behavior of a single child over the course of the semester. Because the observation of one child can serve as a paradigm for observing all children, students are free to choose any child as their "study child." Very frequently, students chose to observe girls and/ or White children. However, after the instructor began to assign the article by Barbarin and Crawford (2006) that reports on the negative ways in which preschool teachers reacted to the behavior of boys of color, there was a notable increase in the number of students who chose to observe boys. It appears that the article served to "prime the pump" in stimulating an interest in the behavior of boys, particularly boys of color. Later, when analyzing their observation notes, many of these students made reference to gender and race/ethnicity and the role it played in adult responses to their study child's behavior.

Another teacher educator used very creative ways to raise student awareness of the role of gender in boys' lives in school. She played James Brown's "It's a Man's World" to a class of undergraduate students in a course on early childhood curriculum and also assigned the task of comparing the reading scores of boys and girls in their locale, an inner-city neighborhood, as well as data on the reading scores of low SES boys and girls. When she subsequently took the class on a field trip to observe in a kindergarten classroom, they were indeed primed to notice differences in the behavior of boys and girls (Wright, 2006).

METHODS FOR OBSERVING AND RECORDING

Although observations can be conducted for very brief durations and still be valuable, it is hard for teachers to stand back from ongoing classroom events even for a few minutes to record what they observe, so it is necessary to deliberately plan in order to accomplish this. In preschool and kindergarten classrooms, where there is typically more than one adult present, it is easier to do so knowing that there is another adult who remains involved in the activities of the moment. Teachers can plan together to schedule regular times to observe so that every child is observed multiple times over the course of the year. However, in the early elementary grades (1–3), where teachers typically work alone, even a 3-minute observation can feel onerous. Teachers can surmount this challenge by selecting contexts in which children are least likely to need their immediate attention— for example, when the class is fully occupied in individual seatwork; when they are with a special teacher for gym, art, or music; or during recess or lunch. Another strategy is to keep a small notepad and pencil handy to jot down interesting events.

There are many different methods that have been developed for observing and recording children's behavior. Three of these (running records, sociograms, and checklists) are described here in some detail. All three can be used to conduct on-the-spot documentation of children's behavior as it occurs. Each is explained along with ways that they can be adapted to specifically explore and reflect on the role that gender expectations and stereotypes may play in young boys' behavior, choices of activities, and in their interactions with peers.

Running records, which require concentrated time to write, are most easily done in pre-K and kindergarten classrooms where other adults may be present to oversee the classroom while one teacher is taking notes. In first through third grade, where teachers typically work alone, checklists and sociograms are very useful because they allow teachers to note information at a glance and still remain engaged in overseeing the class as a whole. Nevertheless, it is worthwhile to strive to conduct running records as well, since they provide the richest information about the "whole" child.

Observation data can also serve as a stimulus for teachers to reflect on their own practices. Are there ways in which classroom structures serve to support stereotypes? Are there ways to intervene so that boys can participate more fully in classroom life freed from their own internalized gender restrictions as well as those of their peers? Observation data can help teachers ponder such questions with a clearer picture of what is actually happening in the classroom.

It is common for teacher educators to give observational assignments to their students, and these can be specifically geared toward reflection on the role of gender in classroom life (Hinitz, 1996). For example, with support from her instructor, an undergraduate student in early childhood education undertook a research study in which she made use of running records and sociograms to record the behavior of boys in classroom settings. During a sedentary activity, she noted that the boy she was observing "rarely sat in his chair but (would) stand next to it or put one of his feet on the chair so that he was semi-leaning onto it." The children were expected to (sit in) their chairs but the teacher did not say anything specifically to him about (his posture). This observation speaks to this boy's need to move and the teacher's capacity to accommodate to that need (Chesney, 2006).

Running record. The running record, also known as the specimen record, is one major technique for observing and recording the behavior of children. The teacher takes a few minutes to sit back and watch an individual boy, recording in as much detail as possible what he says and does and what others (adults and children) say and do who interact with the boy being observed. Although one can never capture all that happens, with practice, teachers get better at recording descriptive details—not just what is said and done, but facial expressions, voice tones, and quality of movements (Cohen, Stern, Balaban, & Gropper, 2008). This method lends itself to reflection about the meaning of the boys' behavior from their perspective. So much of what can be seen as stereotypic male behavior—physical bravado, large movements, disparagement of activities that are seen as feminine—may be evidenced by young boys who are trying on their gender role for size. It is therefore quite important for teachers to gather evidence about the contexts in which boys engage in such behavior and the contexts in which they do not in order to consider appropriate interpersonal and curricular strategies for helping boys develop into successful students and empathic, caring individuals.

What is most important is to avoid characterizing what is observed or the boy's internal state—for example, "When the teacher announced that it was clean-up time, Michael acted angry because he didn't want to clean up," but instead to find descriptive words that create a picture of what was observed, "When the teacher announced that it was clean-up time, Michael frowned and in a harsh tone said, 'No!'".

Furthermore, if the teacher also records the context in which the behavior takes place, it can lend insight into the child's behavior. If Michael's reaction to the clean-up announcement was preceded by his concentrated involvement in the activity at hand, such as building a garage for some toy cars, it suggests that he was still very much involved in what he was doing and perhaps did not feel that his work was finished. This suggests some alternatives that the teacher can consider. Can his building be left in place to be completed at a later time? Can Michael be given some more time to work on the building? If neither is possible, does the teacher have a camera handy to take a photo and suggest to Michael that she can help him re-create it on another day?

A compilation of running records over time can reveal patterns in the behavior of an individual boy, including patterns that reveal gender sensibilities. For example, the following excerpts come from observation notes focused on 3-year-old Jack over a 2-month period. The observer reviewed these notes and selected these three excerpts as examples of behavior where gender identity awareness seems to be at play.

Jack meanders over to Simon and Josh with his two long blocks. He maneuvers one of the blocks so that it is jutting out slightly and he walks forward with it so that it taps the blocks that Simon has just stacked. The blocks scatter. Josh exclaims, "Hey!"

Josh holds a doctor's costume up to the teacher and says, "I want to be the doctor." The teacher helps him put it on. Jack exclaims, "I want to be the doctor!" He stands up and rests his right hand on the shoulder of the teacher, who is kneeling down. He looks longingly at Josh in the doctor's costume and in a tentative and slightly whining tone asks, "When can I have a turn?"

Mark called, "I'm Spider-Man!" and Jack called, "I'm Batman." Mark ran away toward the climber and began to climb up the monkey bars. He called to Jack, "Follow me." Jack seemed to begin to follow him, but then he ran in a circle instead.

Each of these excerpts describes behavior that one might expect to see in any preschool or kindergarten classroom. However, as teachers record the behavior of individual boys over time, certain patterns can begin to emerge. The activities, the play themes, and the gender of peers with whom Jack is interacting suggest that indeed he is making choices in keeping with an emerging gender identity. Although this is not cause for particular concern, it raises certain questions. Does he also choose to interact with girls, or is he excluding them? Does he ever adopt more gender-neutral roles during sociodramatic play? Does he ever take advantage of more sedentary activities during choice times, such as painting or looking at books? If continued observation indicates that Jack's choices are predominantly in keeping with male stereotypes, the teacher can begin to think of ways to encourage him to expand his experiential horizons.

Similarly, a compilation of individual running records of many children can reveal gender-related patterns that otherwise may seem to the teacher to be a matter of individual preference. A group of teachers compared running records of individual boys and girls during choice times when they could engage in active hands-on learning and at other times where they were expected to sit still, such as snack, meeting time, and music. They thought together about whether or not there were any differences in the behavior of boys and girls when they were active or sedentary. They did indeed notice the following gender-related patterns:

- During group meeting times, boys engaged in more apparently restless body movements, such as touching shoes, touching peers, and sucking their shirts, than did girls.
- During sedentary activities that involved eating, boys were focused and less restless than girls.
- During choice times, boys covered more ground in the classroom, while girls stayed in the locale of the choice they selected.
- With some exceptions, girls chose activities where other girls were located and boys chose activities where other boys were located.

Sociogram. In activities where children are given the opportunity to choose the peers with whom they interact, sociograms can provide a quick glimpse of friendship patterns and interest-based groupings (Almy & Genishi, 1979). At a glance, the teacher can record the interactions of children who are in proximity to one another. This observation technique can be adapted to focus on gender and other aspects of identity.

For example, a sociogram was recorded during lunchtime in a class-room made up of 4-year-olds. In this sociogram, two boys, Jamal and Geraldo, chose to sit next to each other. (Jamal is African American and Geraldo is Latino.) Jamal initiated a positive interaction with Geraldo, and Geraldo responded in a positive way. Jamal also initiated a posi-tive interaction with Lila, who is Latina. However, she did not respond. Geraldo initiated a negative interaction with Jessica, a Caucasian girl, who responded negatively. In contrast, the interactions between the two girls were positive (see Figure 7.1).

The information from sociograms recorded on different occasions in different contexts offers a quick way to uncover clues about the role that gender and other aspects of identity may play in boys' interactions. Who do they play with? Who do they talk to? What is the nature of those in-teractions? The patterns that emerge can provide the teacher with new

Figure 7.1. Sociogram: Interactions Among a Small Group of 4-Year-Olds at Lunchtime

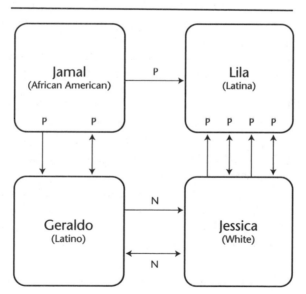

Legend:

P = positive   N = negative

⟶ = initiates interaction   ⟵⟶ = responds

information and a lot of food for thought about kinds of curricular inter-
ventions that may expand children's interactions with peers in positive
ways. For example, Geraldo responded positively to overtures from a
boy named Jamal, but initiated an interaction that was negative with a
girl named Jessica. Jamal initiated a positive interaction with Lila. If a
pattern emerges from numerous sociograms that Jamal typically inter-
acts positively with both girls and boys while Geraldo tends to be more
negative with girls, it could be valuable to assign Geraldo to frequently
sit at the table with Jamal during snack or lunch along with some girls.
If the teacher also sits at the table, she can facilitate positive interactions
and also comment on them when they occur—for example, "Jamal, I
liked the way you thanked Jessica for passing the juice." Geraldo might
then be more likely to imitate Jamal's way of interacting. Geraldo also
could be assigned at times to work with a female partner with attention
paid to the partner being a girl with whom he has had at least some positive interactions.

Table 7.1. Pre-K Classroom Checklist: Participation of Girls and
Boys During Choice Times

Date: March 25	**Age of students:** 4
No. of boys in class: 12	**No. of girls in class:** 10

Activity Choice	Number of Girls Participating	Number of Boys Participating
Block area	1	4
Creative art activity (water color table painting)	3	2
Manipulatives (puzzles)	1	1
Sociodramatic play area (going to the store)	3	0
Listening center	2	2
Library/books	1	0
Other (sand table)	0	3

Checklists. Checklists are another method for observing and recording children's participation in classroom life. This method can be adapted for a wide range of purposes (Almy & Genishi, 1979). It can be used to track individual children's participation in activities over time. It can also be used on any given day to record the boys' and girls' activity choices at a moment in time (see Tables 7.1 and 7.2).

Checklists can be specifically devised to document where boys and girls choose to participate during choice times. For example, in a preschool classroom, typical daily activities available during choice time include blocks, sociodramatic play, painting, manipulatives, a listening center, the library, and a sand table. The teacher can list these in a checklist format and then record the number of boys and the number of girls who choose to participate in each of these activities at the beginning of the work period. If, after a few days or a week of such observations, the numbers indicate that boys predominate in certain areas, such as blocks and manipulatives, but are far less likely to choose the sociodramatic play area or painting, it serves as an alert for the teachers in this classroom to think about how to intervene. Even in first, second, and third grade classrooms, where choice times may occur far

Table 7.2. Elementary Grade Classroom Checklist: Participation of Girls and Boys During Choice Times

Date: April 3   **Grade of students:** 2nd grade

No. of boys in class: 13   **No. of girls in class:**

Activity Choice	Number of Girls Participating	Number of Boys Participating
Board games	2	6
Computer	1	2
Listening center	1	1
Library	4	1
Free drawing	3	0
Other (Feeding fish)	0	1
Other (LEGOs)	1	1

less frequently and where the choices children are afforded are different—
board games, puzzles, or computer games—it is still important to notice if
gender plays a strong role in the areas where children congregate. (See the
strategies suggested in the chapters on social-emotional development, literacy, and active learning through play for ideas about how to intervene.)

USING OBSERVING AND RECORDING
TO BETTER MEET BOYS' NEEDS

The issues raised in the first chapter of this book all point to the challenges
that teachers face in meeting the needs of boys in early childhood classrooms.
In an educational climate so heavily focused on academic performance, a
more holistic view that includes social-emotional and physical development
can be obfuscated. A systematic approach to observing and recording can act
as an antidote by providing teachers with "data" about each boy—his developmental capacities, his interests, his patterns of behavior—all of which can
be used to plan curriculum to better meet boys' needs.

Observation data can reveal how gender stereotypes are played out
in the classroom in ways that put boys at risk. In their efforts to appear
"masculine" or because of their struggles with academics, are individual boys receiving predominantly negative feedback from adults and/or
peers? Are they being treated as if they are troublemakers who need to be
disciplined? What alternatives do the observation data suggest?

No matter how they behave in the classroom, young boys need the
support of nurturing adults. For example, a student teacher illustrated
how teachers might address a boy's social–emotional needs while observing Alan, a first-grade boy, who came from a troubled family. At times
when life was particularly difficult at home, Alan's behavior in school was
observed to deteriorate. For example, one day he failed to participate in
an ongoing whole-group activity and began to display off-task and potentially disruptive behavior. Later, the student teacher and teacher found out
from Alan about an occurrence at home. Alan expressed worry because
his mother's boyfriend, a man prone to physical violence, had recently
recontacted the family. It was Alan's good fortune to be in a class with a
teacher who had formed a relationship of trust with the mother. This un-
doubtedly contributed to Alan's willingness to share this information.

The student teacher's close attention to Alan also appeared to make
a difference. As time went by, Alan increasingly sought her attention, ap-
proaching her upon arrival in the morning and sometimes hugging her.

Alan made fun of a question raised by one of the girls in the class, saying, "That's a 'd' question. That's a stupid question." (To his credit, he made these remarks quietly.) He also preoccupied himself with physical activity, including engaging in a solitary sword fight with two pieces of straw and punching his fists against a piece of furniture. The student teacher who was taking observation notes at the time decided to interrupt her observation by sitting next to him and putting her arm around him to draw him in and calm him as the head teacher continued the activity at hand.

She in turn would greet him warmly and physically respond with a brief hug, intuiting that he needed this kind of physical affection and affirmation. Not only did this serve to meet Alan's emotional needs of the moment, but it also provided a model of nurturance that could expand Alan's view of how adults and children interact and serve to counteract the physically aggressive behavior that he had witnessed at home.

USING OBSERVING AND RECORDING TO INFORM CURRICULUM PLANNING

Observing and recording has long been used for purposes of assessment and curriculum planning. By noticing boys' behavior over time, teachers can gain insight about how to better meet their social-emotional and learning needs.

For example, at the end of the semester, the student teacher who observed Alan came up with a recommendation that reflected the insights she derived from her observations. She hypothesized that his off-task physical activity and solitary dramatic play such as sword fighting enabled him to distract himself from his worries about what was going on at home even though it also served to distract him from the activities at hand. She posited that giving Alan frequent opportunities to engage in drawing, painting, collage, and other kinds of expressive activities were an important emotional outlet, allowing Alan to express his feelings in socially appropriate ways, such as when he drew a figure with razor-sharp teeth and claws or when his "torn collage" art seemed to represent a gun.

There are also many ways to use observation and recording to better meet children's academic needs. A student teacher who observed Zoran, a second-grade boy, over the course of the semester came up with a set of recommendations based on an analysis of her observation notes. She noted that Zoran's handwriting and organizational abilities appeared to be impediments to successful academic performance.

The student teacher also noted that his verbal expressive skills were more advanced than what his writing suggested. Noting that this must be a source of frustration for him, she supported the strategy already in place— that he work on his pencil grip—but also thought that it would be valuable for Zoran to be able to use the computer to get his ideas into written form. Alternatively, he could start with a drawing to express his thinking or dictate a first draft to an adult who could legibly encode his actual words. He could then work with the adult or independently when he was ready to elaborate on these ideas. Once satisfied, he could copy his draft into a final piece with the opportunity to focus on his handwriting, having already gotten his ideas onto the written page in his earlier drafts.

STRATEGIES

At the beginning of the year, develop a plan for systematically observing the behavior of the boys in the class over time. In order to come to know the boys in the class as individuals, come up with a feasible schedule for writing running records and anecdotal observations. It is critical to observe each boy in different contexts and at different times of the day and days of the week to get a full picture.

Use checklists toward a range of purposes. Checklists like those shown in Tables 7.1 and 7.2 offer a quick reading on gendered choices that children make. Other checklists can be devised in order to get to know boys' academic and other strengths, interests, and needs.

Use sociograms to track boys' social interactions. Sociograms like the sample shown in Figure 7.1 can be used to get a picture of boys' social relationships. This can help show which boys are recruited by others and which are not, as well as the boys who take a leadership role in initiating social interactions with other boys and/or with girls.

There were two occasions when Zoran couldn't read his own notes and another where he used correct strategies to solve a math problem but spaced the work on the page in such a way that it became visually confusing, perhaps contributing to his ultimate arrival at an answer that was wrong even though he seemed to understand the problem.

Share recorded observations with parents. Observation data also serve as a rich information source to share with parents during regularly scheduled parent conferences. In addition, when there is a need to meet with parents because of a concern about a boy, it is always reassuring for parents to hear a clear description of their son's behavior rather than a report that jumps to the teacher's reactions, analysis, or expression of concern.

CONCLUSION

There is no doubt that in early childhood classrooms boys suffer from inaccurate and/or harsh judgments when their behavior does not fit with predetermined expectations. These judgments are a disservice and can lead to very negative long-term outcomes. All children yearn to be known as unique individuals and to be appreciated for who they are—their frailties as well as their strengths. As the anecdotal material in this book illustrates, children's behavior always tells a story. It is the job of teachers to try to read that story correctly and refrain from judging the behavior when it doesn't fit with predetermined expectations.

It is critical that teachers be aware of the challenges that boys face during the early years of school. With this knowledge, teachers are in a better position to use observing and recording to come to know their male students as unique individuals and to transform the classroom to better meet their needs.

FOR FURTHER REFLECTION

- What role can the teacher play in facilitating positive interactions among boys and girls in the classroom, so that choice activities do not become the exclusive or primary domain of one gender?
- How can the observation data be used to better meet the needs of each boy in the classroom?
- How can a boy's strengths be used to better meet his needs?

KEY READINGS

Almy, M., & Genishi, C. (1979). *Ways of studying children*. New York: Teachers College Press.

This book provides an overview and specificity about the application of different observation techniques and the value of collecting observation data.

Cohen, D., Stern, V., Balaban, N., & Gropper, N. (2008). *Observing and recording the behavior of young children*. New York: Teachers College Press.

This book provides a detailed view of how running record observations can provide insights about the meaning of children's behavior. It encourages teachers to think about children in developmental terms and as unique individuals whose behavior is shaped by their experiences in the world. Although it is focused on early childhood classrooms where active learning is emphasized, the techniques that are described can also be applied to more traditional, academically focused classrooms.

MacNaughton, G. (2000). *Rethinking gender in early childhood education*. St. Leonards, Australia: Allen & Unwin.

Using examples from classrooms for young children, the author provides many ideas on how to alter everyday practice to promote greater gender equity in early childhood education.

APPENDIX A

Selected Reference Books on Children's Literature

The listings below have been selected to help in the process of engaging boys in reading—especially reading for pleasure. The first annotations are selected reference books on how to find high-quality children's literature, including multicultural titles, books in Spanish, and books about the interests and concerns of children.

Adell, J., & Klein, H. D. (1976). *A guide to nonsexist children's books*. Chicago: Academy Press.

> *One hundred forty-one titles, including books that are no longer in print, are organized by age groups, one of which covers preschool through third grade. Within each age group, the titles are subdivided into fiction and nonfiction. There are annotations for each book.*

Association for Library Services to Children. (2009). *The Newberry and Caldecott awards 2009 edition: A guide to the Medal and Honor Books*. Chicago: American Library Association.

> *Each year, a new issue includes the most recent winners of these two children's book awards, along with a listing of those from past years going back to 1922 and 1938 for the Newberry Award and Caldecott Medal, respectively. Annotations are provided.*

Bowker, R. R. (2009). *Subject guide to children's books in print 2009*. New Providence, NJ: Author.

> *This two-volume edition organizes books by subject and indicates recommended ages for readers. There are no annotations.*

Children's Book Committee. (2008). *Best children's books of the year*. New York: Bank Street College, distributed by Teachers College Press.

> *Recommended books are divided into age groups that include "Under 5" and "5–9." Books are divided into categories relevant to a wide range of interests, including adventure and mystery, animals, beginning readers, fantasy, folk and fairy tales, growing up, humor, history, and sports.*

Coretta Scott King Book Award Curriculum Resource Center. www.TeachingBooks
.net/csk. Retrieved August 28, 2009.

> *Organized by grade range, this is a rich resource for identifying award-winning chil-*
> *dren's books focused on people who are African American. The cover of each book is*
> *displayed, along with a recorded message from its author. Many of the books may be*
> *of particular interest to boys.*

Dreyer, S. S. (1994). *The bookfinder: When kids need books. A guide to children's lit-*
erature about interests and concerns of youth aged 2–18. Circle Pines, MN: American
Guide Services.

> *Annotations are provided for hundreds of children's books and include the recom-*
> *mended age for readers. There are also title, author, and subject indexes; the subject*
> *index includes descriptors that can be helpful in identifying books that may be of*
> *particular interest to boys.*

Lima, C. W., & Lima, J. A. (2006). *A to zoo: Subject access to children's picture books.*
(7th ed.). Westport, CT: Libraries Unlimited.

> *This reference book offers 23,000 picture-book titles that are considered appropriate*
> *for children from preschool through second grade. The book includes a bibliographic*
> *guide, a title index, and an illustration index. The subject guide offers more than*
> *1,200 descriptors, many of which can be helpful in identifying books that may be of*
> *particular interest to boys.*

Miller-Lachmann, L. (1992). *Our family, our friends, our world: An annotated guide*
to significant multicultural books for children and teenagers. New Providence, NJ:
R.R. Bowker.

> *Books are organized into 15 geographic categories, such as the United States, Mexico*
> *and the Caribbean, and East Africa. The United States is divided into ethnic sub-*
> *categories, including African American, Asian American, Hispanic American, and*
> *Native American. Annotations are provided.*

Schon, I. (2004). *Recommended books in Spanish for children and young adults: 2000–*
2004. Lanham, MD.: The Scarecrow Press, Inc.

> *Organized by categories (reference, nonfiction, fiction), annotations are provided*
> *along with recommendations regarding the age of readers.*

APPENDIX B

Engaging Books for Boys

There is both conventional wisdom and research about why boys don't seem to enjoy reading or use it as a pleasurable pastime in the same way that girls do. And there is great concern among parents and educators about the growing gap in boys' literacy skills as discussed in Chapter 4. Much has been written about providing more books in the classroom that boys say they like, and about teachers revisiting the books they select for the classroom library. One caution: In making wider choices available for boys, one needs to be mindful of the literary quality of the books that are selected.

The selections below are meant to serve as guidelines for choosing books geared to boys' interests that also have literary merit. The selections are for boys 3–11 years old and include many picture books with big, bold, colorful illustrations or photographs, and chapter books.

The listings are not exhaustive. They are meant be a catalyst for building a library that is engaging to boys. The criteria for selection are books that:

- Show adult males in responsible and caring roles;
- Are multicultural and respectful of family groupings;
- Depict adult male and female characters in nonstereotyped ways;
- Are high-quality in terms of language and illustration;
- Cover a broad range of fiction and nonfiction topics that research shows are engaging for boys.

Adventure

Adler, D. (2005). *Bones and the dinosaur mystery*. B. N. Johansen (Illus.). New York: Viking.

> *Young Jeffrey Bones does some detective work to find the plastic dinosaur given to him by his grandfather. This is one of a series of easy-to-read adventure/mystery stories for grades 1–3. Other titles include* Bones and the Birthday Mystery, Bones and the Cupcake Mystery, *and* Bones and the Big Yellow Mystery. *Ages 6–9.*

Burton, V. L. (1950*). Calico the wonder horse, or the saga of Stewy Stinker*. V. L. Burton (Illus.). Boston: Houghton Mifflin.

A horse named Calico captures a gang of cattle thieves and turns a Christmas party into a success even for the bad guys. A comic-style, "rootin', tootin'" Western story with lightning bolts and clouds of dust flying. Ages 4–8.

Lester, J. (1998). *Black cowboy, wild horses: A true story*. J. Pinkney (Illus.). New York: Dial Books.

Bob Lemmons, an African American cowboy who was a former slave, is able to corral a herd of wild mustang horses single-handedly. Poetic language and vivid illustrations convey an exciting portrait of cowboy life, including thundering hooves, heat, and dust. Ages 5 and up.

Lester, J. (1994). *John Henry*. J. Pinkney (Illus.). New York: Dial Books for Young Readers.

John Henry is an African American folk hero who has enormous physical strength, a big heart, and a willingness to take on any task. This book is an American legend writ large. Ages 5 and up.

Osborne, M. P. (2008). *Magic tree house: The knight at dawn*. New York: Random House.

This book is part of a series of 25 very popular chapter books featuring a brother and sister who travel through time and have exciting adventures in different historic periods, but always are home in time for school. Ages 7–9.

Thompson, S. L. (2008). *Pirates, ho!* S. Gilpin (Illus.). Tarrytown, NY: Marshall Cavendish Children.

Big, bold illustrations and humorous drawings depict a very funny, diverse group of pirates. Told in verse, the pirates are meant to be fierce and scary, but they are just children at heart. Ages 4–6.

Construction/Machines

Burton, V. L. (1939). *Mike Mulligan and his steam shovel*. V. L. Burton (Illus.). Boston: Houghton Mifflin.

This is a classic story written in the 1930s that still has great appeal for young children. Mike Mulligan and his faithful steam shovel "Mary Anne" are both old, and newer diesel-powered shovels are preferred. But Mike Mulligan says that he and Mary Anne can dig out a cellar for the town hall in one day! They do it, but forget to make a path for getting out of the cellar. With some clever problem-solving by townsfolk, Mike becomes the custodian of the new town hall, and Mary Anne becomes the boiler. Ages 3–4.

Burton, V. L. (1943). *Katy and the big snow*. V. L. Burton (Illus.). Boston: Houghton Mifflin.

This picture book has delighted children since the 1940s. Katy is a big red bulldozer with a snow plow in front. After a big blizzard, she is able to clear all the snow from the town streets in one day. The story makes large machinery accessible and exciting for very young children. Ages 3–4.

Macken, J. E. (2008). G. Saunders-Smith (Consulting Ed.). *Construction zone demolition*. Mankato, MN: Capstone Press.

A book with photographs of all stages of a building being demolished. It shows equipment used for razing a building, talks about how usable objects are recycled, and illustrates how a razed site is prepared for a new building. Explains the meaning of vocabulary related to the topic. Excellent for urban children who see construction sites all around them. Ages 4–8.

Sciezka, J. (2009). *Trucktown: Pete's party*. L. Long & D. Gordon (Illus.). New York: Simon & Schuster.

This is one of a new series of books about vehicles written to appeal to preschool boys. Trucks are the main characters. Ages 3–6.

History/Biography

Adler, D. A. (1991). *A picture book of Martin Luther King, Jr.* R. Casilla (Illus.). New York: Holiday House, Inc.

A picture book that highlights Dr. King's childhood and family, and the legacy of his struggle for racial equality. The book has an unusual amount of factual information for the picture-book genre. Ages 4–9.

Adler, D. A. (2003). *A picture book of Lewis and Clark*. R. Himmler (Illus.). New York: Holiday House, Inc.

An introduction to the lives and Lewis and Clark and their adventures in exploring and mapping unknown parts of North America from St. Louis, Missouri, to the Pacific Ocean. Ages 5–8.

Bearden, R. (2003). *Li'l Dan the drummer boy: A Civil War story*. R. Bearden (Illus.). New York: Simon & Schuster Books for Young Readers.

An African American boy who is a slave works very hard to build himself a drum. Alone in the world as the Civil War rages around him, he is adopted as a mascot by a unit of Union army soldiers. He becomes a hero by warning his unit of nearby enemy fire by playing a rat-a-tat on his drum with drumsticks that he makes from small tree branches. Ages 5–10.

Humor

Horsfall, J. (2003). *Kids' silliest jokes*. B. Jones (Illus.). New York: Sterling Publishers.

Twelve chapters provide a huge repertoire of riddles and jokes for kids to share with their friends and families. Includes bedtime jokes, bathtime jokes, and knock-knock jokes, to name just a few topics. The pages are filled with cartoon-like illustrations. Ages 7 and up.

Scieszka, J. (1992). *The stinky cheese man and other fairly stupid tales*. L. Smith (Illus.). New York: Viking.

> *This book is full of wonderful satire at a child's level. The author uses humor with funny, comic-book-type illustrations to retell children's stories and fairy tales. Everyone who reads them, adults and children alike, laughs out loud. Ages 4–8.*

Thomas, J. (2009). *Rhyming dust bunnies*. New York: Atheneum Books for Young Readers.

> *A colorful bunch of dust bunnies say words that rhyme, and then one of them says a word that doesn't rhyme at all. The other dust bunnies are increasingly annoyed with him because they don't realize that he's warning them that they are about to be vacuumed up! Ages 3–5.*

Zane, A. (2005). *The wheels on the race car*. J. Warhola (Illus.). New York: Orchard Books.

> *A takeoff on the preschool song "The Wheels on the Bus." Bold drawings of racecars that make loud engine sounds are driven by large animals such as a bear, a rhino, and an elephant. Ages 3–5.*

Nurturant Males

Cameron, A. (1981). *The stories Julian tells*. New York: Random House (A Stepping Stones book).

> *A funny chapter book about wild tales that Julian tells his little brother, Huey. The boys have a nurturing dad who cooks lemon pudding, plants a garden, and goes along with the funny stories that Julian tells. An ALA Notable Children's Book and winner of the Irma Simonton Black Award. Ages 6–8.*

Himes, A. G. (1986). *Daddy makes the best spaghetti*. New York: Clarion Books.

> *Daddy is the main caregiver in this family. He picks his little boy up from daycare, they go food shopping together, and Daddy gives him a bath. Then Daddy cooks a spaghetti dinner before Mommy comes home from work. This gentle story about role reversal shows boys that men also can be nurturers. Ages 3–5.*

Palacco, P. (1998). *Thank you Mr. Falker*. New York: Philomel Books.

> *After enduring years of not being able to read and being teased by her classmates, Trisha is helped by her fifth-grade teacher to understand her learning disability and learn strategies that enable her to read. It's an autobiographical story of the author's struggle with dyslexia as a child. Ages 5–8.*

Schotter, R. (2008). *Doo-wop pop*. B. Collier (Illus.). New York: Harper Collins Children's Books.

> *A school janitor who is a former doo-wop singer teaches several shy, loner-type students to sing doo-wop a capella and dance. The janitor practices with the group after school, and they give a terrific performance for the whole school. Ages 5–9.*

Science

Editors of Yes Magazine. (2008). *Robots: From everyday to out of this world*. Victoria, BC: Peter Piper Publishing, Inc.
  A book of photographs and information about robots, including the history of robotics, facts about how they work, robotic games, and their uses in the real world, such as assisting people with disabilities. Ages 5–12.

Gibbons, G. (2008). *Dinosaurs*. New York; Holiday House, Inc.
  This book has brightly colored drawings of dinosaurs, with names and pronunciations. It offers lots of information about fossils, the differences between plant and meat eaters, eggs hatching, nests, and the probable causes of extinction. Good pictures of female and male paleontologists doing field work. There are several pages of facts at the end of the book. Ages 4–9.

Winter, J. (2007). *The tale of pale male*. J. Winter (Illus.). Orlando, FL: Harcourt.
  This is a true story about a pair of red-tailed hawks who build a nest and raise chicks on the window ledge of a New York City apartment building. The hawks hunt small mammals in Central Park to feed themselves and their chicks. When some people who live in the apartment building wanted to get rid of the hawks' nest, many other people rallied to the birds' defense, and the nest was restored. An exciting story that combines nature and advocacy. Ages 4–8.

Sports

Adler, D. A. (1997). *A picture book of Jackie Robinson*. R. Casilla (Illus). New York: Holiday House, Inc.
  This book is a biography of the first African American to play baseball in the major leagues. The story tells of his triumphs and his personal courage in overcoming the barriers of racial prejudice. Ages 7–10.

Gibbons, G. (2000). *My baseball book*. New York: Harper Collins Publishers.
  A book for beginners that tells all about the game of baseball. The multiracial illustrations show boys and girls playing the game and having fun. There is a glossary of baseball terms in the back. Ages 4–5.

Smith Jr., C. R. (1999). *Rimshots: Basketball pix, rolls, and rhythms*. New York: Puffin Books.
  Photographs, vocabulary words used uniquely as part of the graphic design of the book, and bright colors help convey the excitement of basketball and the passion of the players. The author is inspired by his love of the game and makes connections between great playing and art, music, and poetry. Ages 5 and up.

APPENDIX C

Books About Emotions

Learning how to talk about emotions is an essential aspect of positive social-emotional development. Too often, however, boys learn to bottle up some of their emotions at a very young age. The books below have been selected to help boys recognize and express a wide range of feelings, including sadness, exclusion, gender-based teasing, fear, and anger. A skillfully selected story read at class storytime, to a small group of boys anytime, or on a one-to-one basis when an issue arises can serve as a catalyst for discussion of social-emotional topics that might not otherwise be addressed.

Beckwith, K. (2005). *Playing war*. L. Lyin (Illus.). Gardiner, ME: Tilbury House Publishers.
> *A boy absents himself as his friends decide to play war. He reveals that he is the sole survivor of a bombing in his native country, and when he shares his experience with his friends they respond with empathy. Ages 5–8.*

Cohen, M. (2005). *My big brother*. R. Himler (Illus.). New York: Star Bright Books.
> *A boy's older brother becomes a soldier because he can't afford to go to college. The boy tries to take his older brother's place in the family. The text and illustrations convey with authenticity the mixed emotions of the boy and his mother. Ages 5–7.*

Couric, K. (2000). *The brand new kid*. M. Priceman (Illus.). New York: Doubleday.
> *New, foreign, different-looking Lazlo has to endure teasing and exclusion in his new school, until one girl decides to befriend him and helps others see him as a friend, not a stranger. Interesting illustrations show a lot about body language. Ages 4–6.*

De Paola, T. (1979). *Oliver Button is a sissy*. T. De Paola (Illus.). San Diego, CA: Harcourt Brace & Co.
> *Oliver does not like to do the stereotypical things associated with being a boy. He is happy to get his exercise by tap dancing. Although it is painful for him, Oliver withstands the teasing he encounters in school. After he appears in and almost wins a talent show, Oliver's schoolmates call him a "star" instead of a sissy. Ages 4–6.*

Frame, J. A. (2003). *Yesterday I had the blues*. C. Gregory (Illus.). Berkeley, CA: Tricycle Press.
> *An African American boy describes all the feelings that he and his family experience. He describes his moods by color—blue is feeling low and sad, red is angry, green is*

feeling good—and optimistic words are used poetically, but the story is about every-
day activities to which children will relate. Ages 5–8.

Hooks, B. (2008). *Grump/groan/growl.* C. Raschka (Illus.). New York: Hyperion Books for Children.

A bad mood is on the prowl! Brightly colored, large child-like drawings illustrate bad-
mood feelings, and how to let go of them. Ages 3–8.

Kinney, J. (2008). *Diary of a wimpy kid: Roderick rules.* New York: Amulet Books.

Kinney, J. (2009). *Diary of a wimpy kid—the last straw.* New York: Amulet Books.

The newest titles in a series of "Wimpy Kid" books. Written as a daily diary with a comic-
book layout, this series appeals to boys and other struggling readers. The diaries, about a
middle school boy whose behavior is not the model of stereotypic masculinity, addresses
boys' insecurities and inner feelings in a true-to-life and humorous way. Ages 8 and up.

Krensky, S. (2007). *Big bad wolves at school.* B. Sneed (Illus.). New York: Simon & Schuster Books for Children.

Rufus likes to do "wolf" things such as tumble around and howl at the moon. When
he gets to school, his "wolf" is too active and does not fit in, until his special abilities
are appreciated. Ages 5–7.

Leaf, M. (1936). *Ferdinand the bull.* R. Lawson (Illus.). New York: Grosset & Dunlop.

Ferdinand, who is big and strong and bred for the bullring, refuses to fight. He prefers
to sit under a cork tree and smell the flowers. This classic children's story shows that
you don't have to fit the male stereotype to enjoy life. Ages 4–7.

Lionni, L. (1989). *Frederick.* L. Lionni (Illus.). New York: Scholastic.

Frederick is a mouse who refuses to do stereotypical male things. He prefers to be
quiet, contemplative, and artistic. His being different causes resentment in his com-
munity—until the value of his gifts are discovered. Ages 4–5.

Minshull, E. (2005). *Eaglet's world.* A. Gabriel (Illus.). New York: Albert Whitman & Company.

This book addresses the fear of change that many young children experience through
the story of a young male eagle who has to learn to leave the nest. His parents coax
him to the edge of the nest, but he is afraid to take his first flight into the big world
beyond. Finally, he does it successfully. Ages 4–8.

Sendak, M. (1963). *Where the wild things are.* New York: Harper and Rowe.

Imagination, fantasy, and mythological creatures help Max, a little boy who has misbe-
haved and been sent to his room without dinner, work through his feelings of fear and
anger. This beautifully written and illustrated book, which won the Caldecott Medal in
1964, conveys emotions that are often difficult for boys to express. Ages 4–8.

Spelman, C. (2004). *When I feel scared.* K. Parkinson (Illus.). New York: Albert Whitman & Company.

A story with comforting words and illustrations to help young children address fears.
The main character is a bear who is afraid of many things but learns some strategies
to make himself feel better. This book was cited in the 2003 edition of Best Children's
Books of the Year by Bank Street College. Ages 3–5.

Viorst, J. (1989.) *Alexander and the terrible, horrible, no good, very bad day.* New York: Scholastic.

> *On a day when everything goes wrong for him, Alexander is consoled by the thought that other people have bad days, too. This book provides opportunities to talk about how angry feelings can spill over and affect your day, and to problem-solve nonaggressive ways of expressing and managing them. Ages 4–6.*

Warner, G. (2004). *Benny's boxcar sleepover.* New York: Albert Whitman & Company.

> *Benny and his friends very much want to have a sleepover in the boxcar that sits in his grandfather's backyard. When night falls, the boys begin to feel scared and creep back into the house in the dark. The question is—do they actually spend the night in the boxcar? Ages 6–8.*

Yashima, T. (1976). *Crow boy.* New York: Puffin/Penguin Books.

> *Set in a small Japanese village, this book tells the story of Chibi, an isolated child who is taunted by his peers and made out to be the class clown. When in sixth grade he displays a remarkable talent for imitating the language of crows, he is given the name Crow Boy. His classmates finally realize that they have been unkind and never took the time to get to know Chibi as a friend. This Caldecott Honor Book provides opportunities to discuss the hurtful effects of teasing and bullying. Ages 5–9.*

Zolotow, C. (1989). *William's doll.* W. P. Du Bois (Illus.). New York: Harper Trophy Edition.

> *This story addresses gender stereotyping in a way that has engaged young children since it was first published in 1972. William is taunted and teased by his brother and his brother's friend because he wants a doll. His father offers William "boy things" every time he asks for a doll. But his grandmother understands, and explains that William wants a doll so he can practice being a father. Ages 3–5.*

References

Almy, M., & Genishi, C. (1979). *Ways of studying children*. New York: Teachers College Press.

Andersen, M., & Hysock, D. (2008). *Thinking about women: Sociological perspectives on sex and gender* (8th ed.). Boston: Allyn & Bacon.

Barbarin, O., & Crawford, G. M. (2006). Acknowledging and reducing stigmatization of African American boys. *Young Children, 61*(6), 79–86.

Barros, R., Silver, E. J., & Stein, E. K. (2009). School recess and group classroom behavior. *Pediatrics, 123,* 431–436.

Benard, B. (2004). *Resiliency: What we have learned*. San Francisco: WestEd.

Berk, L. E. (2003). *Child development* (6th ed.) Boston: Allyn & Bacon.

Bodrova, E., & Leong, D. J. (2003). The importance of being playful. *Educational Leadership, 60*(7), 50–54.

Bowman, B., & Moore, E. K. (Eds.). (2006). *School readiness and social-emotional development: Perspectives on cultural diversity*. Washington, DC: National Black Child Development Institute.

Bridges, S. B. (1993). Pink or blue: Gender stereotyped perceptions of infants as conveyed by birth congratulations cards. *Psychology of Women Quarterly, 17,* 193–205.

Bruner, J. (1969). *Toward a theory of instruction*. Cambridge, MA: Harvard University Press.

Chesney, J. (2006). Research on the crisis in boys' education. Unpublished paper.

Chu, J. Y. (2000). *Learning what boys know: An observational and interview study with six four-year-old boys*. Unpublished doctoral dissertation, Harvard University, Cambridge, Massachusetts.

Cohen, D., Stern, V., Balaban, N., & Gropper, N. (2008). *Observing and recording the behavior of young children*. New York: Teachers College Press.

Collaborative for Academic, Social, and Emotional Learning. (2007). Background on social and emotional learning. *CASEL briefs*. Retrieved August 31, 2009, from http://www.casel.org/downloads/SEL&CASELbackground.pdf

Comer, J. P. (2005). Child and adolescent development: The critical missing focus in school reform. *Phi Delta Kappan, 86,* 757–763.

Conference on Minorities in Special Education. (2001). Harvard Civil Rights Project, March 2001.

Copple, C., and Bredekamp, S. (2009). *Developmentally appropriate practice in early childhood programs: Serving children from birth through age 8.* Washington, DC: National Association for the Education of Young Children.

Day, C. B. (2006). Leveraging diversity to benefit children's social-emotional development and school readiness. In B. Bowman & E. K. Moore (Eds.), *School readiness and social-emotional development: Perspectives in cultural diversity* (p. 31). Washington, DC: National Black Child Development Institute.

Dewey, J. (1938). *Experience and education.* (60th Anniversary edition with a new preface by Dewey issued in 1998). New York: Macmillan.

Elkind, D. (2006). *The power of play: How spontaneous, imaginative activities lead to happier, healthier children.* Cambridge, MA: De Capo Press.

Epstein, A. S. (2009). *Me, you, us: Social-emotional learning in preschool.* Ypsilanti, MI: High/Scope Press.

Epstein, J., Sanders, M. G., Sheldon, S. B., Simon, B. S., Salinas, K. C., & Rodriguez-Jansorn, N., et al. (2009). *School, family and community partnerships: Your handbook for action.* (3rd ed.). New York: Corwin Press.

Fagot, B. (1978). The influence of sex of child on parental reactions to toddler children. *Child Development, 49,* 459–465.

Feldman, R. (2008). *Language, literature, and emergent literacy.* New York: Bank Street College of Education, unpublished course syllabus.

Ferguson, A. (2000). *Bad boys: Public school in the making of black masculinity.* Ann Arbor: University of Michigan Press.

Flood, C. (2000). *Raising and educating healthy boys.* Concept Paper. New York: Educational Equity Concepts, Inc.

Garbarino, J. (1999). *Lost boys: Why our sons turn violent and how we can save them.* New York: The Free Press.

Gartrell, D. (2006). Guidance matters: Boys and men teachers. *Young Children, 61*(3), 92–93.

Genishi, C., & Dyson, A. H. (2009). *Children, language and literacy. Diverse learners in diverse times.* New York: Teachers College Press.

Gilliam, W. S. (2005). *Prekindergarteners left behind: Expulsion rates in state prekindergarten programs.* Foundation for Child Development, Policy Brief, Series No. 3.

Ginsburg, K. R. (2007). The importance of play in promoting healthy child development and maintaining strong parent-child bonds. *Pediatrics, 119*(1), 184.

Goleman, D. (1995). *Emotional intelligence: Why it can happen.* New York: Bantam Books.

Greenberg, S. (1985). Educational equity in early childhood environments in S. Klein (Ed.), *Handbook for achieving sex equity through education* (p. 457). Baltimore: Johns Hopkins University Press.

Gropper, N. (2004). *Raising and educating healthy boys: Analysis of focus groups held with teachers and parents in urban and suburban settings.* New York: Educational Equity Concepts, Inc.

Gurian, M., Henley P., & Trueman, T. (2001). *Boys and girls learn differently*. Hoboken, NJ: Jossey-Bass.

Halle, T., Calkins, J., Berry, D., & Johnson, R. (2003). Promoting language and literacy in early childhood care and educational settings. *Child Care & Early Childhood Education Research Connections*. Retrieved October 19, 2009, from http://www.childcareresearch.org

Hamre, B. K., & Pianta, R. C. (2007). Learning opportunities in preschool & early elementary classrooms. In R. C. Pianta, M. J. Cox, & K. L. Snow (Eds.), *School readiness and the transition to kindergarten in the era of accountability* (pp. 49–83). Baltimore: Paul H. Brookes.

Hawkins, J. D., Kosterman, R., Catalano, R. F., Hill, K. G., & Abbott, R. D. (1999). Promoting positive adult functioning through social development intervention in childhood. American Medical Association. *Archives of Pediatrics & Adolescent Medicine, 153*, 226–234.

Henderson, A., & Mapp, K. L. (2002). *A new wave of evidence: The impact of school, family, and community on student achievement*. Austin, TX. Southwest Educational Development Laboratory (National Center for Family & Community Connections with Schools).

Hinitz, B. (1996). Guiding the learning experiences of young children: A course in early childhood education. In E. G. Freidman, W. K. Kolmar, C. B. Flint, & P. Rothenberg (Eds.), *Creating an inclusive college curriculum: A teaching sourcebook from the New Jersey Project* (pp. 263–269). New York: Teachers College Press.

Hyde, J. (2005). The gender similarities hypothesis. *American Psychologist, 60*(6), 581–591.

Hyson, M. (2003). Putting early academics in their place. *Educational Leadership, 60*(7), 20–24.

Kafele, B. K. (2009). *Motivating black males to achieve in school & in life*. Alexandria, VA: ASCD.

Katz, J. (1999). [Online video]. *Tough guise: Violence, media and the crisis in masculinity*. Available from Media Education Foundation [http://www.mediaed.org].

Keyser, J. (2006). *From parents to partners: Building a family-centered early childhood program*. St. Paul, MN: Redleaf Press.

Kimmel, M. (2000, November). What about the boys? *WEEA Digest*, 1–8.

Kindlon, D., & Thompson, M. (1999). *Raising Cain: Protecting the emotional life of boys*. New York: Ballantine Books.

King, M., with Gartrell, D. (2004). Guidance with boys in early childhood classrooms. In D. Gartrell, *The power of guidance: Teaching social-emotional skills in early childhood classrooms* (pp. 106–124). Clifton Park, NY: Delmar/Thomson Learning.

Klass, P. (2009). Conference presentation. *Educational equity: Global and national strategies*. Institute for Health and Social Policy. McGill University. Montreal, Canada, May 2, 2009.

Koch, J., & Irby, B. (Eds.). (2002). *Defining and redefining gender equity in education.* Greenwich, CT: Infoage Publishing.

Kohl, H. (1994). *I won't learn from you: And other thoughts on creative maladjustment.* New York: New Press.

Kohlberg, L. (1966). A cognitive developmental analysis of children's sex-role concepts and attitudes. In E. E. Maccoby (Ed.), *The development of sex differences* (pp. 82–173). Stanford, CA: Stanford University Press.

Lynch-Brown, C., & Tomlinson, C. M. (2005). *Essentials of children's literature.* Boston: Pearson.

MacNaughton, G. (2000). *Rethinking gender in early childhood education.* St. Leonards, Australia: Allen & Unwin.

Mead, S. (2006). *The evidence suggests otherwise: The truth about boys and girls.* Washington, DC: Education Sector.

Meisels, S. (2007). Accountability in early childhood: No easy answers. In R. C. Pianta, M. J. Cox, & K. L. Snow (Eds.), *School readiness and the transition to kindergarten in the era of accountability* (pp. 31–47). Baltimore: Paul H. Brookes Publishing.

Miller, E., & Almon, J. (2009). *Crisis in the kindergarten: Why children need to play in school.* College Park, MD: Alliance for Childhood.

Newkirk, T. (2003). The quiet crisis in boys' literacy. *Education Week, 23*(2), 34.

Newkirk, T. (2005, October 12). "Brain research"—A call for skepticism. *Education Week.* Retrieved December 26, 2006, from http://www.edweek.org/ew/articles/2005/10/12/07newkirk.h25.html?qs=Newkirk.

Pender, R. L. (2009). *Boys and girls respond differently to literacy: An international study analyzing the differences in gender literacy preference.* Unpublished manuscript.

Piaget, J. (1954). *Construction and reality in the child.* New York: Basic Books.

Pianta, R. C., Cox, M. J., & Snow, K. L. (Eds.). (2007). *School readiness and the transition to kindergarten in the era of accountability.* Baltimore: Paul H. Brookes Publishing.

Pollack, W. (1998). *Real boys: Rescuing our sons from the myths of boyhood.* New York: Random House.

Porche, M. V., Ross, S. J., & Snow, C. E. (2004). From preschool to middle school: The role of masculinity in low-income urban adolescent boys' literacy skills and academic achievement. In N. Way & J. Y. Chu (Eds.), *Adolescent boys: Exploring diverse cultures of boyhood* (pp. 338–360). New York: New York University Press.

Raider-Roth, M. (2003, April). *Knowing their journey: Understanding the complexities of teaching boys, a documentary account.* Paper presented at the American Educational Research Association Annual Conference, Chicago.

Raider-Roth, M. B. (2005). *Trusting what you know: The high stakes of classroom relationships.* San Francisco: Jossey-Bass.

Richardson, L. (1988). *The dynamics of sex and gender: A sociological perspective.* (3rd ed.). New York: Harper & Row.

Riley, D., San Juan, R. R., Klinker, J., & Ramminger, A. (2008). *Social & emotional development: Connecting science and practice in early childhood settings.* St. Paul, MN: Redleaf Press. (Taylor & Machida, p. 99; Reynolds, p. 99; Flouri & Buchanan, p. 99).

Rosenfeld, M. (1998, March 26). Little boys blue: Reexamining the plight of young males. *The Washington Post*, p. 1.

Rubin, J. Z., Provenzano, F. J., & Luria, Z. (1974). The eye of the beholder: Parents' views on sex of newborns. *American Journal of Orthopsychiatry, 44,* 512–519.

Scherer, M. (Ed.). (2006). Teaching to student strengths. *Educational Leadership, 64*(1), 8–16.

Schickedanz, J. (1999). *Much more than the ABC's: The early stages of reading and writing.* Washington, DC: National Association for the Education of Young Children.

Schon, D. (1983). *The reflective practitioner: How professionals think in action.* New York: Basic Books.

Schweinhart, L. J., & Weikart, D. P. (1997). *Lasting differences: The HighScope preschool curriculum comparison study through age 23.* Ypsilanti: MI: High/Scope Press.

Serbin, L., Conner, J., & Citron, C. (1978). Environmental control of independent and dependent behaviors in preschool boys and girls: A model for early independence training. *Sex Roles,*1(6), 867–875.

Shaffer, S. M., & Gordon, L. P. (2000). *Why boys don't talk and why we care: A mother's guide to connection.* Chevy Chase, MD: Mid-Atlantic Equity Consortium, Inc.

Shepard, L. A., & Smith, M. L. (Eds.). (1989). *Flunking grades: Research and policies on retention.* London & New York: Falmer Press.

Smith, F. (1988). *Joining the literacy club: Further essays into education.* Portsmouth, NH: Heinemann.

Smith, R. A. (2002). Black boys: The litmus test for "No Child Left Behind." *Education Week, 22*(9), 40, 43.

Smith, R. A. (2003, November/December). Race, poverty, & special education: Apprenticeships for prison work. *Poverty & Race, 12*(6), 1–4.

Snow, K. L. (2007). Integrative views of the domains of child function: Unifying school relations. In R. C. Pianta, M. J. Cox, & K. L. Snow (Eds.), *School readiness and the transition to kindergarten in the era of accountability* (pp. 197–216). Baltimore: Paul H. Brookes Publishing.

Thorne, B. (1994). *Gender play: Girls and boys in school.* New Brunswick, NJ: Rutgers University Press.

Tyre, P. (2008). *The trouble with boys: A surprising report card on our sons, their problems at schools, and what parents and educators must do.* New York: Crown Publishers.

Unger, R., & Crawford, M. (1992). *Women and gender: A feminist psychology*. New York: McGraw-Hill, Inc.

U.S. Department of Education. (2003). Office of Special Education Programs. *25th Annual Report to Congress*. Washington, DC: Author.

U.S. Department of Education. (2004). Trends in educational equity of girls and women. Washington, DC: Author. Retrieved July 1, 2009, from http://nces.ed.gov/pubs2005/2005016.pdf.

Viadero, D. (1998, May 13). Their own voices. *Education Week*, 34–37.

Wright, D. (2006). *Boys' literacy development*. Unpublished manuscript.

Zaman, A. (2007). Raising and Educating Healthy Boys: Paternal Acceptance and Rejection. Panel Presentation at AACTE, February 25, 2007.

Zehr, M. (2009). Authors share tips on how to hook boys on books. *Education Week*. Retrieved July 11, 2009, from http://www.edweek.org/ew/contributors/mary.zehr.html.

Index

About the Authors

Barbara Sprung is co-director of the Educational Equity Center at AED. From 1982 to 2004, she was cofounder and co-director of Educational Equity Concepts. A graduate of Sarah Lawrence College, she received an M.S. in child development from the Bank Street College of Education, and is a graduate of the Institute for Not-for-Profit Management, Columbia University. Formerly an early childhood classroom teacher, Ms. Sprung has an extensive background as a developer of nonsexist, multicultural, and inclusive educational materials. Having written extensively, she is the author of *Nonsexist Education for Young Children* (1975) and edited *Perspectives on Nonsexist Early Childhood Education* (1978). Most recently, she coauthored *The Anti-Bullying and Teasing Book* (2005).

Merle Froschl is co-director of the Educational Equity Center at AED. From 1982 to 2004, she was cofounder and co-director of Educational Equity Concepts. She holds a B.S. in journalism from Syracuse University and is a graduate of the Institute for Not-for-Profit Management, Columbia University. Ms. Froschl has extensive experience in education and publishing and has developed outstanding curricular and teacher training models in the field of educational equity. She is a nationally known speaker and has published widely. She is coauthor of *The Anti-Bullying and Teasing Book* and the chapter on early learning environments in the second edition of the *Handbook for Achieving Gender Equity through Education* (2007, S. Klein et al., Eds.)

Nancy Gropper is a faculty member and co-chair of the Department of General Teacher Education at Bank Street Graduate School of Education. She received both her Ph.D. and M.A. from Teachers College, Columbia University, and her B.A. from the University of Delaware. Prior to coming to Bank Street, she was a faculty member at Brooklyn College, City University of New York, and at the State University of New York at New

Paltz. She was formerly an early childhood classroom teacher. Dr. Gropper
has extensive experience as an evaluator of educational programs. Among
her publications are articles focusing on gender issues, and she recently coauthored the fifth edition of *Observing and Recording the Behavior of
Young Children* (2008).